Body and Soul

Teams, Trust and Transformation

Robert Gernon

Detselig Enterprises Ltd.

Calgary, Alberta, Canada

Body and Soul
© 1999 Robert Gernon

Canadian Cataloguing in Publication
Gernon, Robert, 1947-

Body and soul
ISBN 1-55059-189-4

1. Teams in the workplace. 2. Personnel management. I.
Title. HD66.G47 1999   658.3'128   C99-910179-X

Detselig Enterprises Ltd.
210-1220 Kensington Rd. N.W.
Calgary, Alberta T2N 3P5
telephone: (403) 283-0900 / Fax: (403) 283-6947
e-mail: temeron@telusplanet.net
www.temerondetselig.com

Detselig Enterprises Ltd. appreciates the financial support
for our 1999 publishing program, provided by Canadian Her-
itage and other sources.

Printed in Canada
ISBN 1-55059-189-4
SAN 115-0324

Cover design by Dean Macdonald

Dedication

To Reta and George
With Love and Gratitude

Many, Many Thanks

This book could never have been completed without the support and encouragement of many dozens of people over the past 20 years. I cannot possibly thank you all by name, but there are several that I simply must, so here goes:

- Fred Kaiser, John Crawford, Robert Tsang and Terry Green at Honda.
- Nancy Littlewood and Mike Nestor at The Toronto Transit Commission.
- Dimitri Chrus, Connie Marcello and Debbie Gomm at *The Globe and Mail*.
- Doug Smith, Roger Harris and Paul Keelan at Famous Players.
- Charlotte Gibson and Ev Loring at The Heart and Stroke Foundation.
- Mike Tracy at Universal Superabrasives.
- Dan McGrath and Darlene Stewart at Cineplex Odeon.
- Kathy Elliot-Bryden and Doug Matheson at Seneca College.
- Scott Catfield and Bill McKim at the Ontario Municipal Management Institute.
- Ed Hardison and Ralph Suppa at the Canadian Institute of Plumbing and Heating.
- Jane Lackner and Norm Hamfelt at Trans-Canada Pipelines.

Final Thanks to my Writing, Editing and Critiquing Teams:

- John Reynolds, Sharon Gernon, Alan Davey, Elizabeth Davey, Dan McGrath, Darlene Stewart, Paul Keelan, David Geldart, Mieke Geldart, Judy Sibbitt, Sandra Margeson, and of course Linda and Ted at Detselig.

Thank you! Thank you! Thank you!

Table of Contents

Testimonials

John Bennett – FlightSafety Canada

Having worked with Bob now for over a year, we believe we are much more productive and efficient managers. We have a team with a sense of self, a corporate culture which is evolving to include more employees in the decision-making process, and a clearly-defined mission and purpose to aim for. Have we succeeded? . . . In our case, what we are practicing makes so much sense, and what we gave up seems so contrary to what we know people can accomplish, that we are happy to be where we are. We would invite other management teams to join us in this voyage of self discovery.

Bob Lord – Technical Equipment

I have worked with Bob Gernon for seven years on a variety of projects. . . . Having had great success in using his program elsewhere, we have begun using his system at our machine tool distribution company to weld our organization into a team that is focused on serving our customers and exceeding their expectations.

The parts of Bob's program that I like best are the simplicity of the concepts and the way they empower everyone in our company to serve our customers, make decisions and contribute to continuous improvement. His methods really harness the innovative power of everyone in the organization and help to accelerate company progress on numerous fronts. . . .

The program is simple and easy to use. It makes a great deal of obvious sense and can be modified for personal preferences or specific situations to achieve the needed result. Any team member, from the chairman to office clerks, administrative workers or sales people, can derive a great deal of benefit from these systems.

David Thomas – Trimax Retail Systems

Over the past three years, Bob has provided and contributed to Trimax Inc. the following:

- *Good understanding of effective organizational structures.*
- *Good understanding of team dynamics and team values.*
- *Demonstrated the strength of a team is greater than any effort of a single individual.*
- *Illustrated the organization expectations from the role of the President.*

Trimax could not have matured and grown to where we are today without his thoughts, leadership and guidance.

Mike Tracy – Universal Superabrasives

I have worked with Bob Gernon for 10 years in several businesses. . . . We have been able to outperform our competitors in this period and I credit Bob for the considerable contribution he has made to our success. Bob has helped us really understand and realize the massive potential present in all people . . . all we needed was the tools to create teams and teach our folks how to work together.

Bob has brought a unique group of skills to the table, from leadership training to detailed sessions on communication, facilitation, listening skills and many more.

The investment in changing our culture has been significant for us, but the payback has been one of the best that we have seen! I recommend this way of management . . . it works!

"The greatest change of all is probably that in the last forty years, purposeful innovation – both technical and social – has itself become an organized discipline that is both teachable and learnable."

Peter Drucker, 1996
Managing in a Time of Great Change

Introduction

Things are out of whack. Like a spinning top that loses its stability and begins to wobble off its axis, the North American business culture is growing less steady, less effective and less rewarding day by day. It may be a reflection of current society or it may be an impetus to changing cultural values. It doesn't matter. Corporate culture in North America has, with few exceptions, never been more indecisive and less focused than in the late 1990s.

Why? Let's begin with some familiar aspects of Doing Business on the Cusp of the Millennium:

- Constant Change: We're all undergoing incessant change. In fact, we're learning to live with the idea of perpetual change. The problem is, we're still not very good at managing it.

- The Incredible Shrinking Organization: Downsizing used to be something a company would have to apologize for, like a fuel spillage or an inaccurate advertisement. Now it's a process to boast about. The pride that a CEO once took in creating 1000 jobs is nothing compared to the satisfaction the same CEO might take today in downsizing by the same number of jobs. Is the new goal of corporations to shrink themselves in incremental stages until they disappear? Is this what Carnegie, Ford and Rockefeller had in mind?

- Sleight of Hand or Just Out of Hand?: Many companies claim to be more profitable when they have simply transferred the wealth from one sector to another. They manage to generate the same amount of gross income from a small group of employees, paying them less in salaries and benefits. The savings are passed on to shareholders as larger dividends, increasing the company's share price and enhancing the stock option plans of its senior executives. If we didn't need a weatherman to tell which way the wind is blowing, do we need a Karl Marx to tell us something is a little out of whack here?

- Four Seasons or Four Crops per season?: Senior executives, some of whom wouldn't know they were on a farm if they tripped over a combine, are suddenly thinking like farmers – that is, in strictly quarterly seasons. The difference is that these executives want a record harvest each quarter, even though farmers know that you only get one harvest season a year. The drive to show a new record in every quarter continues. If farmers thought like these executives, they'd want to bring in four wheat crops a year. Yet, no matter when you sow your seeds, you still get one crop per year, and everything you do should be focused on enhancing the yield of that crop – on the farm and in the board room.

- Whither the corporate soul? All of this indicates to me that business executives are missing an element of their lives, their skills and their job functions that few have addressed until now: it's their centre, their moral compass, *their sense of a soul* which exists beyond the board room and has an impact beyond this quarter's bottom line.

Many people, on both ends of the political spectrum, may be astonished to discover a business book dealing with topics like ethics and morality – especially one written to assist companies and their executives in implementing value-enhancing change.

"Morality, ethics?" I can hear some on the Left giggle. "Isn't 'Ethical Business' an oxymoron?"

"Morality?" those on the Right may sneer. "That's something you deal with in church, not in a hard-nosed decision-making arena like day-to-day business."

They're both wrong. Morality has long been a basic factor in any successful business venture that seeks to grow beyond corner-store status.

Lose your moral compass and you risk losing an affinity with, and appreciation for, the lifestyle of the overwhelming majority of your customers.

Abandon an abiding sense of Right and Wrong, Fair and Unfair, and you may succeed as a short-term flash in the pan but you're doomed as a long-term business visionary.

I'm not suggesting that the senior executives of major corporations are immoral. But I am suggesting that the changes made in corporate restructuring since the end of the "Can't Lose" 1980s have come at a price few have examined.

And the price is a loss of something called "**Soul**."

For a moment, for one brief enlightening moment, step out of your role as a business executive or a manager, or even as a capitalist seeking to harvest your share of the benefits of a free-enterprise society, and ponder some examples of things whirling out of whack, losing their centre and wobbling on their axis.

Consider this one:

Michael Jordan is a gifted athlete, a major basketball star and generally regarded as a fine human being. Michael Jordan is paid $20 million annually – that's $55 000 per day, 365 days a year – to wear Nike shoes.

Nike is a very successful company. They are acknowledged as a leader in their field, producing high-quality innovative products for a clearly-defined audience. The Nike shoes as worn by Michael Jordan sell for about $75 per pair and are manufactured in offshore plants in countries such as Indonesia.

Indonesia is a heavily-populated country struggling to rise from third world status and become an industrialized nation, able to provide for its citizens. The Indonesian factory worker who builds Michael Jordan's shoes – the ones he is rewarded at a rate of $55 000 per day to keep either on his feet or in his locker – is paid $4.76* per day. Still, he or she is marginally better off than workers performing similar services for Nike in Vietnam where the average pay is $1.00 per day.

---

*David Olive, *Report on Business*, August 27, 1996, p. B7

Or to put it another way:

Over 50 000 Vietnamese workers building shoes that Michael Jordan wears don't make as much money as he does simply by wearing them.

Michael Jordan deserves to earn as much as he can through his efforts, whether they involve dribbling a basketball or wearing shoes. Nike Shoes deserves to make a reasonable profit, and if that includes seeking the lowest-cost labor force, so be it. And both Indonesia and Vietnam deserve an opportunity to develop their industrial base, whether it's by making athletic shoes or computer parts.

But don't you get a sense that something strange is going on here?

Don't you wonder just how long this extreme of wealth and poverty can exist before some sort of strain develops?

Don't you wonder how greedy you have to be to spend $55 000 a day . . . or how poverty-stricken you must be to survive on $1.00 a day?

There's more:

An American business executive goes to Japan, rents a car and visits a gas station. Immediately, five young men in uniforms surround his car. They check the oil, wash the windows, pump the gasoline, polish the lights and even clean the tires. The businessman pays a high price for the gasoline, partially because gasoline prices in Japan are strictly controlled to limit consumption. "This is outrageous!" the businessman grumbles.

A week later, the same businessman is in New Jersey. He stops to pump his own gasoline, which is priced much lower than not just Japan, but anywhere else in the industrialized world. Nearby, a cashier sits inside a security cage, a Colt .45 at her elbow as five young men in uniforms – hooded sweatshirts, baggy pants and Michael Jordan shoes – surround the businessman's car. They are not there to clean his windows or fill his tank with gasoline. They are there because they have no jobs – even one as basic as pumping gas and wiping windows – and no one cares to offer them such a job because it would raise the price of gasoline. As the young men approach the businessman, the woman in the cage reaches with one hand for the telephone to call the police, and with the other for her gun. "This is outrageous!" the businessman says.

When the police investigate the mugging, when the courts judge and sentence the young men, and when the young men serve their terms in prison, the businessman's taxes pay for it all. But his gasoline remains cheap . . .

Forgive me for sounding overly cynical about these situations, but they reveal a disturbing picture – one which needs to be addressed, admittedly, by all of society. As a management consultant dedicated to assisting corporations in their adjustment and management of change, however, I believe they reflect – in the business context at least – a serious problem which, if it is not rooted in corporate values, is reflective of and influenced by them.

Yes, society must change. I doubt if there is a corporate leader in North America who will disagree with the basis of that statement. But the majority of them will also say: "That's not my job!?" Ah, but it is!

More revealing anecdotes:

Business executives everywhere will tell you they don't enjoy laying off or firing their staff. Only a sadist would. But if there was no joy in conducting the following layoffs, ask yourself how much pain was felt on the part of the released employee – and how easily it might have been reduced had the company demonstrated an affinity with basic human values:*

A 23-year employee of a Massachusetts hospital was called into her supervisor's office and told she was being released in favor of a younger, less expensive employee. Shaken, she returned to her desk . . . to find the new employee already seated there, doing her work.

A candy factory in New England announced that it was closing, and that all employees were now un-employed, by releasing the news to local television stations first. Most em-

---

Boston Globe, June 10, 1996

ployees – some who had been with the firm for 30 years or more – discovered they had no jobs while eating dinners with their families, watching the evening news.

An employee with a brokerage firm was called into her boss's office where she was informed over a speaker phone, by a Human Resources manager in the New York office, that she no longer had a job.

Workers at a Texas oil company turned up for work one morning to discover a fleet of taxis waiting outside their office building. Boxes with the employees' names written on them, containing the employee's personal effects, were inside the cabs, and the employees were instructed to get in the cabs and return home – they were out of a job. "They were all screaming and crying," said the out-placement consultant who was called in to deal with the damage.

Let's assume each of these layoffs was "justified" to some extent by economic conditions of one kind or another. Let's also assume that the executives responsible for these fiascoes are not essentially evil people. The point is, these disturbing events needn't have happened at all, and *a corporation with as much soul as it has bricks and mortar would ensure not only that these disasters were avoided but that everyone – company, employees, executives and shareholders – could benefit in some way by the circumstances.*

That's what I have determined over many years of studying corporations, both admirable and not so admirable, as a consultant focusing on change management. I have seen corporations face challenges, develop a strategy of change to meet those challenges, generate wide support to implement and measure the strategy, and emerge stronger, more vital and more confident than ever. I have been honored to help them do it.

Most important, I have recognized that they all shared one common element: A sense of identity, a system of values, an awareness of moral values . . . or, in a word, a *soul*.

You can't install a soul as though it's new computer software. But you can instill one as a consequence and a by-product of change. If the soul of a corporation is alive and well, and if the management of the company is able to implement change effectively, the company will survive and prosper even through the most demanding times.

You doubt it? All right, here's an example:*

The Xerox Corporation has been admired for its management ability virtually since its inception in the 1950s. During the late 70s the firm lost its way a little. More important, it lost half its market share (the two events were, of course, directly connected). During the 1980s, Xerox was faced with making one of two sharply contrasting decisions: Take "The Low Road" and slash jobs, close plants and shrink its scope to match its market share; or take "The High Road" and find a way to create jobs for existing people.

Xerox management realized that the company had always attracted bright, capable people – people whose talents and experience represented the company's most valuable single asset. The High Road meant tapping this knowledge and nurturing the latent creativity of the employees. Before they could apply this asset, they had to deliver security to the employees – otherwise, why would the employees share their knowledge?

Once Xerox employees realized they wouldn't be turfed out onto the street, they didn't care what job they were working on. The company literally looked into its soul, assessed its strength, plotted a strategy of change, and reassigned work according to the strategy. The employees quickly began applying their knowledge and experience in a myriad number of ways and, by the end of the decade, Xerox had regained its market share.

See? There is an alternative to The Low Road, and while taking The High Road may not be easy, it's far more beneficial and satisfying in the long run.

Throughout my career and in the text that follows, I have identified aspects of a corporate soul and defined ways of nurturing it among management and employees alike. Then I married these techniques with a step-by-step plan to imple-

---

*Harper's Magazine: May, 1996

ment change in order for these deeply-rooted corporate values to emerge as part of the change process.

To borrow a phrase from a totally different kind of author, let's <u>Stop the Insanity</u>. Let's eliminate the idea that the only way to deal with a corporate challenge is to rid it of experienced employees.

Let's nurture the one corporate quality that aids a firm's ability to change above all others: a sense of commitment and identity on the part of its employees.

Let's blend the sense of corporate soul with the mechanics of a proven method of implementing change.

That's what this book is about.

"We are souls with bodies, not bodies with souls."
Pierre Teilhard de Chardin

Preface

The more things change . . . the more people write books about it. Well, that's one way to view the challenge of personal and organizational change with which we are faced today.

I set out to write a book about change within human organizations. Whether they be companies, governments, teams or families, all human organizations share certain similarities.

They have a body, i.e., some kind of structure. It could be hierarchical or totally egalitarian, but every organization must have a structure and it is this structure or architecture that defines the rules for relating, communicating, problem solving, decision making, sharing the rewards and meeting all the needs the structure is set up to satisfy.

But having a body, even an efficient, slim, trim, muscular, sexy body, isn't enough.

All humans and their organizations need a soul.

So I set out to write a book that would share my experiences with some of the "why to's" and "how to's" for friends, colleagues and clients who are in the process of building their own lives, their relationships and especially for those who are attempting to positively impact the Body & Soul of the organizations within which they live and work.

Over the years, supported by evidence and instinct, I developed the belief that the basic process of life (personal and corporate) is meant to be an upward and outward journey of continuous change and growth, conducted with a conscious will and a deep regard for the welfare of others.

By definition, in this life, change is inevitable and continuous. So it seems logical that it ought to be something at which every individual and organization should work deliberately to become expert.

While change may be inevitable, unfortunately improvement is not. In fact, it is my contention that improvement as a direct result of change is positively abnormal. Those who paid attention in their physics classes may recall the Second Law of Thermodynamics, which states: "Left on their own, all things move towards chaos." (If you were paying more attention to popular music than physics in the 1970s you might also recall Paul Simons' lyric: Everything put together, sooner or later falls apart. Same thing.)

What we need – and what this book is about – is a recognition that work, our work, the work of living growing human beings needs to be defined as: "The process by which we bring order out of chaos." That's the central thesis of all the change theories and management techniques people have been talking and writing about since the mid 1980s.

Bringing order out of chaos begins by making a commitment to constant improvement – a commitment that is triggered by a quiet, internal decision based on high level value judgments and leading to a life-affirming leap of faith.

That's the bright and positive side of change that I hope to describe in this book. Unfortunately, change has another side. Sometimes it is motivated by dark and destructive forces. Forces that produce turmoil and decay. We'll need to deal with that side too. And we'll also explore some of the laws and principles that govern change, the consequences of ignoring those laws, and the need for a level of stability, in the midst of the change process, that is attainable only through a sense of being centred, balanced and rooted in reality.

At the core of this book, I hope you'll discover a source of hope. Not hope based upon immature fantasy and self-delusion, but hope based on truth, wisdom and conscious choice. Only this kind of hope will lead to a firm decision to seek constant improvement, and only this kind of hope will support the commitment necessary to sustain it.

I have spent the last five years assembling all that I have learned and applied in management training and corporate change over the past 25 years. In spite of all the time and energy I had devoted to learning about change, I still hesitated to produce this book because a vast library on the same topic was already available to owners, executives and managers trying to negotiate their companies through the rip-tides of change. But three things changed my mind.

The first was the truly exhilarating experience of developing a simple but not simplistic process for managing change and watching it prove effective in my own life and with my clients. It made sense to document the system in a readable manner.

The second was the recognition that *we have underestimated the breadth, depth and impact of (corporate) change on society.* In the words of a corny old song, "We've only just begun." If you have grown weary of change as a corporate goal, I'm sorry to say "you ain't seen nothin' yet!" (Almost as sorry as my grade eight grammar teacher would be if he saw that sentence.) Day by day, all of us are discovering new ways in which it is affecting every aspect of our lives from board room to bedroom. Inundated as we are in messages about change, we cannot and will not escape it. All we can do is deal with it in as painless a manner as possible . . . and it is my hope that this book may help some to even turn it to their advantage.

The third reason was the clincher for me, for while there are many books on change, none, to my knowledge, deal with the duality I intend to explore as a central theme . . . that as humans we were created "souls with bodies" and it is from this perspective that we must create our organizations.

Organizations are human creations and if they are to thrive they must have souls first and then bodies which mirror and act out their values.

Form Follows Function
A word about the organization of this book

This book has been written by a practitioner of change for other practitioners. It is not a book of theory, but it recognizes that all effective practice must be based on sound theory.

The first 80% of this book is meant to be motivational, inspirational and directional in nature. Each chapter is intended to tell a story about some key principle of change or explode a dysfunctional myth that hobbles or blinds us to the positive potentials that surround us.

The final 20% of this book is prescriptive in nature and outlines a Step-By-Step Process that I have <u>successfully</u> introduced to organizations throughout North America. I am convinced that I learn as much and often more from failure as I do from success, so in this section I will address those lessons I've learned in the hope that those who read these pages will not have to learn from their own mistakes but will profit from mine.

You will also notice several additional design features in this book:

1. The split-page layout. The right side of the page contains the text while in the left-hand column I have included short, pithy and sometimes poetic quotations that are intended to punctuate, reinforce or in some way illuminate the content covered in the text. My intention is that this layout will satisfy the needs of both sides of the brain, i.e., left-brain linear and analytical, right-brain conceptual and creative.

2. The white space. It is my hope that you will use the white space on each page to personalize the content by adding your own thoughts, reactions and intentions.

3. The "Big Ideas." At the beginning of each chapter I have included a brief summary of the "Big Ideas" I intend to cover in the text. There are many other ideas in each chapter, of course, and I recognize that as the reader you are a partner with me and have every right to learn whatever you want or need to learn from the reading process.

My hope is that these design features will enhance the quality of your reading experience by making it clearer what my intentions were at the time of writing and providing you with ample space and opportunity to think about, make notes about and apply the various concepts presented.

4. The Activities. It is my belief that *"The great goal of education is intelligent action."* This section asks you to think, discuss, plan, apply or in some other way take action to put what you know to work.

"To know and not to do is not to know."

Japanese Proverb

CHAPTER 1

Big Ideas

"Beliefs preceed behaviors." So what beliefs will lead to positive change?

Life is not linear. Everything is connected to everything else, so where does one begin a book about change? I thought the best place to begin would be with the individual who is both the subject and the object of change.

Big Idea #1: "The person best positioned to identify and solve a problem (i.e., to make a positive change) is the person closest to that problem."

As I worked with this idea, I came to see it as a basic universal principle that supports the fundamental value and ultimate personal responsibility of the individual. This cornerstone principle is essential to the effective functioning of any human organization.

And yet individuals must act with others ("No one is an island.") if they hope to accomplish much of value.

Big Idea #2: "The total contribution of a well balanced team is greater than the sum of its parts."

This dichotomy and paradox are the heart of what this chapter and this book are about. How can we create communities (teams, families, organizations, churches) that unleash the creative potential of the individual while at the same time honoring and championing that synergy which is the core strength of every great community?

CHAPTER 1

The Best Problem Solver is . . .

Let us ask ourselves as we arise each morning, "What is my work today?" We do not know where the influence of today will end. Our lives may outgrow all our present thoughts and out dazzle our dreams. God puts each fresh morning, each new chance of life, into our hands as a gift, to see what we will do with it.

Anna R. Brown Lindsay

Great minds don't think in straight lines.

Well begun is half done.

If you wish to know the road up the mountain, ask the person who goes back and forth on it.

Zenrin

I began my work experience in one of the toughest training arenas imaginable: a struggling steel mill located far from the industrial heartland of North America. The company was run as a no-nonsense, what's the bottom-line operation. It was also the core industry in a strong union town. Conflicts between management and union were the norm, and any change in the company or its fortunes created a ripple of waves that touched virtually every resident and every other business in the community.

I was following in my father's footsteps. My dad began his working career prior to WW II with the same company. Starting as a laborer, he rose steadily to Electrician, then Foreman, and finally General Foreman, responsible for the maintenance operations of two rolling mills. You can imagine the dirt-under-the-fingernails knowledge my father acquired over all those years, and the wealth of practical insight he possessed about the steel mill's operation. As a young boy I idolized my Dad and I assumed that mill management would consult him whenever it was making any kind of decision regarding the plant's operation.

I was shocked to discover they did not. In fact, one of his great frustrations

Responsible citizens in a democracy who own property, educate children, own and operate businesses, elect and represent one another to government positions should never have to hang their brains at the door when they show up to work.

Pride only breeds quarrels, but wisdom is found in those who take advice.
The Bible Proverbs 13:10

Quality means . . . fit for use.
Quality is defined by the customer.
Quality is the right balance of . . .
• Price
• Availability
• Specifications
• Timeliness
• Service

To seek Quality is to seek Balance.

He that walketh with the wise shall be wise.
The Bible, Proverbs 13:20

was that they rarely even seemed to consider the idea.

And they should have. Because they desperately needed help. Running the mill profitably was not an easy matter for the owners and managers. Through the 60s competition grew more fierce; modernization of equipment became a capital-intensive necessity; environmental, quality, safety, health and human rights concerns demanded attention from employees, community and government; and the mill's fortunes were even more subject to the ebb and flow of good and bad times than similar mills in heavily-industrialized areas.

The prevailing rule I learned during those years was: "Production is #1." Everything else is a distant second. For a while, after the war and into the mid-60s, the climate encouraged this rule. If a sub-standard run of steel was produced, it was simply sold at a cheaper price to a customer who placed a low priority on quality. But in the 70s when the climate began to change – when low-quality customers dropped off like pterodactyls – management was unable to navigate the change because they continued to believe the myth that they could sell whatever they produced and at a handsome profit.

I watched leadership at all levels try to deal with the challenge of raising quality levels while reducing costs and I noted that management rarely, if ever, consulted my father and his colleagues. Yet *they* knew how to do it (at least

Knowledge Is Power.

Proximity Is Perception

Blessed is the one who finds wisdom, the one who gains understanding, for she is more profitable than silver and yields better returns than gold. Wisdom is more precious than rubies, and nothing you desire can compare with her.

The Bible,
Proverbs 3:13-15

some of it) – *they* recognized many of the barriers and could identify potential solutions because they lived with them daily. This awareness revealed something very basic – something obvious to everyone who worked among the dust and ashes yet seemed invisible to the upper management where the floors were carpeted in wool and inlaid with wood. It was:

The person best positioned to identify and solve a problem is the one closest to that problem.

Proximity is perception, and perception leads to knowledge.

Unfortunately, in the case of my father and his generation, rarely did it lead to power.

Of all the insights we carry through the current maelstrom of global changes in business and life, none is more important than the recognition that knowledge is the most valuable asset any organization can possess – more valuable than the buildings and real estate they inhabit, more valuable than their common and preferred shares traded on the stock market, more than the goodwill they carry on their books, and even more than the inventory they retain in their warehouses.

A corporation wastes knowledge at its peril, and as this book unfolds I will present a detailed formula for tapping, organizing and applying that knowledge to produce tangible benefits for all.

Proximity Is Perception At Levi Strauss (1)

For over 60 years, the Levi Strauss company made their famous Model 501 jeans with copper rivets at all points of stress — including a lone rivet at the crotch. In those days, there was little opportunity for buyers to complain about design flaws, and the vast majority of 501s were purchased by macho cowboys. Still, a simple but critical design flaw persisted: When cowboys wearing 501s crouched too long beside the campfire the crotch rivet, located next to the most sensitive part of a cowboy's anatomy, grew uncomfortably hot. In 1933, Walter Haas Sr., Levi president, went camping in his 501s. Crouching by the campfire in the High Sierras one night, the howl of distant coyotes was suddenly drowned by a cry of pain from Haas — he had fallen victim to the Hot Rivet syndrome. Upon his return to Levi headquarters in San Francisco, the copper crotch rivet was banished forever — much to the relief of long-suffering cowboys.*

From the steel company I entered the teaching profession. I also got addicted to volunteer work, community activism and leadership. In the early 1970s, I served two terms as a city councilor and later accepted a position as Program Development Officer in a community college. One of my duties at the college included designing and leading management seminars. I enjoyed and was challenged by this aspect of my job

---

*From *Everybody's Business — The Irreverent Guide to Corporate America* (Moskowitz, Katz & Levering), Harper & Row (New York), 1980

None of us
is
as
smart
as
all of us.

Wisdom is knowledge
which has become a part
of one's being.
Orison Swett Marsden

Many people dream and
hope for success. To me,
success can be achieved
only through the re-
peated use of the three
tools of . . . failure, intro-
spection and courage.
Soichiro Honda

to such a degree that in 1981 I left the college to become a freelance training consultant.

About 18 months later I was fortunate to meet Fred Kaiser and John Crawford of Honda Canada. As we began working together, it slowly dawned on me that Honda's style of management reflected what I had first concluded at the steel company:

The person best positioned to identify and solve a problem is the one closest to the problem.

I had understood this principle in relation to operating heavy machinery or expediting steel orders. But Honda appeared to apply it everywhere, integrating it so deeply into their management practice that it became literally intuitive. But they did something more. They enhanced the strengths of the individual through the team concept. And they applied both concepts effectively, not by totally empowering loose canons to fire in all directions of their own accord, but by creating a system of integrated leaderships that recognized the reality that "the total contribution of a well-balanced team is greater than the sum of the individual parts." Or to put it another way – "None of us is as smart as all of us."

Over the next decade, I worked closely with Fred, John, Richard Green, Robert Tsang and their colleagues at Honda on numerous projects. One of the most successful was created to improve their customer service process.

In 1982 Honda's customer service was ranked 7th among all competition; by 1986, after the program had been implemented, it rated #1.

Applying many of the principles used successfully in customer service improvement, I became involved in their Acura Division. Here we had a clean slate – an almost unprecedented opportunity to implement these principles from the very beginning in a brand new company.

At the start of the year, Acura had no approval rating in customer service because the division occupied no position in the market. But by the end of the first year of operation, Acura dealers actually nudged their Honda cousins out of first place for customer service among new car dealers.*

From there we moved to the task of altering the customers' view of a new car salesperson. We developed extensive training programs to help sales staff change from professional order-takers to customer-centered consultants. Along with these training programs, we worked with Barry Hults and his team at the School for Promotional Marketing in Canada to design and initiate new reward systems to reduce attrition and provide a sharper focus on goals.

By the way, Honda did not call their program "Total Quality Management," and at the time I knew little of

Plans fail for lack of counsel, but with many advisers they succeed.
The Bible, Proverbs 15:22

THE 7 PRINCIPLES OF THE HONDA WAY:

1. *Proceed always with ambition and youthfulness.*
2. *Respect sound theory.*
3. *Develop fresh ideas.*
4. *Make the most effective use of time.*
5. *Enjoy your work and always strive to brighten your working atmosphere.*
6. *Strive constantly for a harmonious flow of work.*
7. *Be ever mindful of the value of research and endeavor.*
   Soichiro Honda

---

*J. D. Power & Associates, 1987

Edwards Deming or Joseph Juran. We just called it "The Honda Way." No one questioned or analyzed it, because it worked. And it worked because no one doubted its two basic premises:

1. The person best positioned to identify and solve a problem is the one closest to the problem.
2. The total contribution of a well-balanced team is greater than the sum of its parts.

Honda did not articulate their philosophy with these words, but they remained at the heart of the company's success and represented what I have come to call "the soul" of the corporation.

With this background and experience, I was able to refocus my leadership training and consulting activities more precisely. Working with my wife and partner we defined our process and mission to:

MY MISSION:
Discover . . .
Master . . .
Share . . .
Bob Gernon

1. Discover the principles and practices of personal and organizational excellence.

2. Master these in our own lives.

3. Share them with others who aspire to excellence.

From this foundation we began working with a broad range of organizations in fields as diverse as public transportation and services, pipelines, computers, film distribution, government, fundraising and volunteer services and more. In most cases, these organizations had already achieved substantial levels of success. They produced high quality products and services and they were staffed and managed by skilled people who believed in what they were doing.

We were usually invited in because somehow these results were not what they might have been. In several cases a fog-bank of impending doom could be sensed in the air, drifting in from the far horizon, even though the immediate situation may have looked quite positive.

Later in this book we'll examine some of these experiences and discover that in every case of successful transformation these two fundamental principles were to be found at the core of the improvement . . . 1) The person best positioned, and 2) The total contribution of a well balanced team is greater than the sum of its parts.

There is nothing so abundant as undeveloped human potential.

Repetition is the mother of memory.

Proximity is Perception at American Airways (3)

In the 1930s, American Airways (now American Airlines) president La Motte Cohu was plagued with numerous complaints about lost airline luggage. Nothing he tried to do seemed to solve it. Finally, he had every American station manager flown to New York for a meeting . . . and arranged to have their luggage lost in transit. The lost passenger luggage problem disappeared almost immediately.*

The moral of the story is . . .

Repeat anything often enough and it will start to become you.
Tom Hopkins

**Everybody's Business*

1. The person best positioned to identify and solve a problem is the one closest to that problem.
2. The total contribution of a well balanced team is greater than the sum of its parts.

ACTIVITIES

I hear and I forget. I see and I remember. I do and I understand.
Chinese Proverb

1. Do you believe in these basic principles? Are they consistent with your experience? If yes, record at least one experience that confirmed each principle for you.

_____

_____

_____

_____

_____

_____

_____

_____

_____

Who is the wise man? He who learns of all men.
The Talmud

2. How do you incorporate these principles into your current management practice? List 3 examples of habits or practices.

_____

_____

_____

_____

_____

_____

_____

_____

The words printed here are concepts. You must go through the experiences.

Carl Frederick

3. What opportunities exist for you to increase the application of these principles?

CHAPTER 2

Big Ideas

**Big Idea #1: Change is impersonal
but its impacts are not.**

**Big Idea #2: Every organization has a mythology that
either helps or hinders it as it attempts to adapt to or
change the environment in which it functions.**

To understand organizations we must understand mythologies and how they work.

CHAPTER 2

Body and Soul

The universe is one great kindergarten. Everything that exists has brought with it its own peculiar lesson. The mountain teaches stability and grandeur; the ocean immensity and change. Forests, lakes and rivers, clouds and winds, stars and flowers, stupendous glaciers and crystal snowflakes – every form of animate or inanimate existence, leaves its impress upon the soul. Even the bee and ant have brought their little lessons of industry and economy.
        Orison Swett Marsden

The unexamined life is not worth living.
        Socrates

The unlived life is not worth examining.
        Anonymous

Events tend to repeat themselves. The tide of opportunity comes to us all. And when we are prepared for opportunity, our chance is sure to come. Success doesn't depend upon being at the right place at the right time – it depends upon being ready.
        Wynn Davis

One morning in Calgary, Alberta, I was preparing myself for a day's work when I glanced at the morning newspaper over breakfast. One of the stories concerned the remains of an ancient dinosaur found in the Bow Valley not a mile from where I sat. I walked to the window and looked out at the panoramic view of the Rocky Mountains in the distance and the valley between us, visualizing those monsters roaming the land over 100 million years ago.

These beasts dominated the world for a period much longer than we can trace the history of humans and all we can find now are their bones. They grew extinct, as far as science can tell us, because they could not adapt. Things changed – the climate, the food chain, the ability of other creatures to outwit them.

My proximity to this discovery helped me to crystallize a new insight about change... "Change is impersonal but its impacts are not."

There was nothing malicious about the change that wiped out those dinosaurs. Tragic, perhaps – especially if you were an emotionally sensitive and upwardly mobile *Brontosaurus*. A sudden change in atmospheric climate – the prevailing theory for the extinction of the dinosaurs – is not a vindictive act.

It is totally neutral, totally impersonal. *But its effects are neither.*

Some organizations and species survive and prosper, while others wither and die in the same climate. Why? What makes the difference? That was the question I asked myself, staring out at the dinosaur graveyard. And then it came to me . . . the difference could be explained, at least partly, by mythology. Let me explain . . .

Every human and organization operates on the basis of a mythology that guides him / her / it.

I don't want to be too anthropomorphic here, but we could say that those dinosaurs operated on the erroneous mythology that things (the climate) would continue pretty much as they had the past few hundred million years.

That mythology or underlying set of beliefs formed a quite functional operating paradigm until that day when the snow began falling in southern Alberta all those centuries ago.

Myths, I think, are to human and organizational behavior what a computer's operating system is to its software. It provides the architecture and power to make sense of the software and allows that software to function effectively i̲f̲ they are compatible.

Since myths and mythologies can be barriers to change, they sometimes prevent us from exercising one of the key differences between humans and dinosaurs: *As humans, we have the ability to*

I think luck is the sense to recognize an opportunity and the ability to take advantage of it.
Samuel Goldwyn

Myths are the operating systems of the soul.

Experience has taught me this, that we undo ourselves by impatience. Misfortunes have their life and limits.
Michel Eyquem De Montaigne

alter our behavior and adapt to the prevailing conditions; or alternatively to influence the environment and make it more favorable to ourselves.

Humans have the capacity to:
1. Change themselves to fit the environment.
2. Change the environment to better fit themselves.

Whenever either personally or through a story in the press, I encounter a corporation which is apparently incapable of change, I think of that massive pile of bones in the Bow Valley and I wonder . . . why?

We can all appreciate the power of organizational, cultural and corporate myths. Those of us who have sought change within a framework of myths that effectively nullify change have felt frustration, anger and a sense of opportunity lost.

Anger is a blocked goal.

It's time, I believe, not only to slay the beasts of myth, but to replace them. But with what? With a system of values that recognizes not only the need for tactics, strategies and measures, i.e., a body, but also with the human quotient in enterprise, a soul. I'm proposing a moral standard for organizations that nudges the pendulum away from one end of its arc, where it swings totally towards bottom-line performance, in the opposite direction where corporations pursue ethical behaviors and practices in tune with human and spiritual needs as well. I am proposing we pursue a <u>life enhancing balance</u>.

Pursue a life enhancing balance.

No, that's not the view of some left-wing socialist survivor, battling the realities of global competition. I am a sincere supporter of a mixed-free-market economy. In fact it is my contention that this is the only way that <u>lasting</u>

SOUL

The immaterial essence, animating principle, or actuating cause of an individual life.

Webster's Ninth

SOUL

The quality that arouses emotion and sentiment.

Webster's Ninth

The only true measure of success is the ratio between what we might have done and what we might have been on the one hand, and the thing we have made and the thing we have made of ourselves on the other.

H. G. Wells

<u>success</u> can be achieved in any economy.

I am deeply concerned that most of today's corporations have lost touch with their human element, *and that loss has cost them their souls.* Whatever your definition of "soul" may be, it is an indispensable element in every conscious being. Lose your soul and you lose your identity. Sacrifice your soul and you sacrifice your primary reason for living a conscious life. Ignore your soul and you ignore the other half of your being – we are, after all, "body and soul."

Western corporations have spent a decade shaping, slimming, trimming, sculpting and restoring their bodies.

Those who ignore their souls do so at the risk of ignoring the source of both the means and direction needed to grow, to change and to prosper.

True success, lasting success, cannot exist until individuals and organizations develop a life, a set of values and a schedule which reflect the need for a balance between a healthy body and soul.

ACTIVITIES:

1. The major Big Ideas for me in this chapter are:

   a) ....

   ....

   b) ....

   ....

   c) ....

   ....

Knowledge conquered by labour becomes a possession – a property entirely our own.
                    Samuel Smiles

2. What is the character or condition of the soul of your organization?

....

....

....

....

....

....

....

....

....

3. List evidence that supports the conclusions recorded in #2. Be specific.

....

....

....

....

....

....

....

....

....

....

CHAPTER 3

Big Ideas

Big Idea #1: Myths exist at the core of every human organization

Big Idea #2: Myths guide and control personal and group behavior

Big Idea #3: Myths are based on thinking and if we want to change our myths from dysfunctional to empowering we must ensure that they are based on truth and rational thought.

CHAPTER 3

Changing Corporate Mythology

Bean counters are doomed.

Work is the process by which we bring order out of chaos.

Oh, I suppose there will always be a place for bottom-line short-term earnings specialists in business – perhaps even a necessary and important place too. But the age of the corporate bean counter as king, spawned early in the 1980s, is in the final stage of death. After all, when you've down-sized, trimmed-back, laid-off and grown lean-and-mean, and you still can't satisfy your earnings level, something is wrong that's above the bottom line. Way above it.

Greatness consists in seeing what everyone else is seeing and thinking what no one else has thought.

The concept of the bean-counter as final arbiter – or, if you prefer, as the power-source emphasizing short-term profits as a measure of corporate strength – is proving to be a modern corporate myth. And corporate myths are as prevalent and powerful in companies as they are in societies, cultures and families.

Myths can be educational, magical, sometimes practical and often universal. Every society and sub-culture creates its own myths, usually variations on existing fables with a regional twist.

A myth is a traditional story of ostensibly historical events that serves to unfold part of the world view of a group or explain a practice, belief or natural phenomenon.

Like the fire-breathing beasts that inhabit many of these tales, myths are difficult to ignore and even more difficult to slay.

This wouldn't be a problem if myths provided us with wisdom beyond dis-

A myth is a popular belief or tradition that has grown up around somebody or something.

A myth often embodies the ideals and institutions of a society or a segment of a society.

A myth is an unfounded or false notion.

Change is the price of health.

Dysfunction – that which acts to inhibit or destroy the primary purpose.

pute, giving us an insight into universal truths that guide us through life. Some cultural myths do. But many don't. Myths are too often considered basic truths when they are actually fanciful descriptions of something that never was. Tragically, corporate myths frequently grow to become formidable barriers that must be circumvented by organizations intent on achieving change. Like a host-killing virus, myths often endure even as the organization which spawned it succumbs. Slay a myth, such as "The Japanese are culturally superior in their management practices," and two new ones pop up in their place. "Japan is a country which acts like a corporation," and "The Japanese are like automatons" spring to mind.

Is there at least a grain of truth to this basic myth and its two offspring? Of course there is. Do they represent reality more than fantasy? I don't think so.

Myths are valuable when they serve to explain our place in the world as individuals, as organizations and as societies. *What leaders don't need is a fantasy posing as a reality. These become negative or dysfunctional myths. Negative myths in turn become barriers to change at a time when change is the only path to life and health.*

That is the danger of unchallenged dysfunctional myths. Especially when they are used as substitutes for rational thought.

"Well I think by this time my staff, my young group of executives, and everybody

else, are convinced that Walt is right. That quality will out. And so I think they're going to stay with that policy because it proved that it's a good business policy. Give the people everything you can give them.

All things noble are first impossible.
Thomas Carlyle

Keep the place as clean as you can keep it. Keep it friendly, you know. Make it a real fun place to be. I think they're convinced and I think they'll hang on after . . . as you say . . . well . . . after Disney."

Walt Disney

This quote from Uncle Walt states his philosophy about how he wanted to serve his guests and has become a defining element in clarifying the Disney culture and mythology.

Truth is adherence to reality. Reality is defined by universal principles.

Keep it Clean . . .

Keep it Friendly . . .

Make it a Real Fun Place to be . . .

The idea for this book was born several years ago when I began conducting seminars to aid corporations in dealing with change. Over and over again, I encountered various negative self-destructive corporate myths. Some were specific to my client companies while others seemed universal. All produced the same result: Deep, inbred resistance to change.

Nature never deceives us; it is we who deceive ourselves.
J. J. Rousseau

Change makes people uncomfortable. That's a given, and it's understandable, even logical. None of us enjoys feeling uncomfortable, and all of us deserve as much comfort in this life as we're capable of providing for ourselves. Unfortunately, comfort isn't necessarily beneficial for us. Couch potatoes who munch potato chips and

All resistance to change is based on fear of the unknown.

The best way to over-come fear of the dark is . . . turn on a light.

A muscle, an emotion or a talent never exercised will atrophy, i.e., What you don't use, you lose.

The real cost of television is not the price you pay for the set but for all those hours of watching it.

GI = GO

Quality Input
+
Quality Process
=
Quality Output

quaff beer while watching somebody spin letters on a game show are very comfortable. But are they healthy? (Or even conscious?)

Remember that *comfort costs*. A little bit of discomfort, like jogging around the block, is one price we can pay for lounging on the sofa. Heart attacks and strokes are another price for enjoying the same pleasure. Which can you afford most?

It wasn't simply a stubborn or lazy resistance to change that explained the difficulty we had when attempting to assist our clients through the process of implementing new systems or re-engineering outdated methods. It was usually a sincere and deeply-held belief in some corporate mythology, which almost everyone in the organization, at every level, instinctively understood and to which they adhered.

There was rarely anything unique about the corporate myths I encountered, either. I have heard them in companies small, medium and gigantic in size, with domestic and foreign ownership, selling everything (literally) from picture tubes to popcorn. The universal nature of these myths and characters proved what every student of mythology knows: *that the same tales, characters and lessons pop up in the mythology of different cultures.*

You already know many of the more common negative corporate myths by their titles or opening lines:

"That won't work here."

"We do things differently."

"We already tried that."

"Only men need apply."

"You have to be tough and uncompromising."

"Why re-invent the wheel?"

"If it ain't broke . . . don't fix it."

"No news is good news."

"Leave 'well enough' alone."

"Don't rock the boat."

"We can't afford the risk."

How do we root out dysfunctional thinking?

Step 1: Recognize it!

Step 2: Replace it!

Where do Dysfunctional Myths come from? They are born in the dysfunctional, negative and irrational thinking patterns which all of us have learned over the years.

To help us sort out what is functional and effective from that which is dysfunctional it is helpful to become familiar with three broad categories of thinking. Let's tackle the negative first. There are two common forms of negative thinking that can lead to dysfunctional beliefs and mythologies.

Number one is <u>irrational thinking</u>. Irrational thinking is based on lies and distortions of the truth. Irrational Thinking = Telling Yourself Lies. e.g.,

"Familiarity breeds contempt."

"You can't fight city hall."

"Things around here will never change."

Three Steps to Making Things Better:
1. *See It as It Is.*
2. *See It Better than It Is.*
3. *Make It Better.*
J. Rohn

Nature understands no jesting. She is always true, always serious, always severe. She is always right, and the errors are always those of man.
Johann Wolfgang Van Goethe

Truth does not contradict truth.
Elizer Zul Zwelfel

Number two is <u>rationalization thinking.</u> Rationalization = Telling Yourself what makes you feel better . . . for now (short term), e.g., "I didn't want that job anyway."

The third and only effective or functional process is <u>rational thinking</u> = Telling yourself the truth. But what is truth? Truth is adherence to reality and reality is defined and determined by the long term generalized principles and laws of life.

What I have learned from doing battle with myths over the years is that: *Myths are champions of durability. If they were metal, they would be titanium. If they were mountains, they would be the Himalayas.*

You don't destroy negative corporate myths easily. *But you can disempower or replace them with rational system-based reasoning founded on today's reality instead of yesterday's fantasies — reasoning that is capable of explaining a group's place in the culture to every member of that group, at every level in the organization.*

You can replace the appeal of corporate myths with the power of shared beliefs and values in your organization's "corporate soul," *creating a concept of organizational sanctuary where every member feels both stimulated and secure in their position and recognition.*

And you can achieve all of this by altering the perception of everyone who plays a critical role in the implementation of corporate change. How? By implementing a logical Step by Step process developed and tested by myself and the people whose stories comprise the second half of this book.

ACTIVITIES

Return to the root and you will find the meaning.
Sengstan

1. What are the two or three most powerful myths in your organization?

   a) ....

   b) ....

   c) ....

The farther backward you can look, the farther forward you are likely to see.
Winston Churchill

2. Are these myths based on rational thinking, irrational thinking or rationalizations?

   a) ....

To know and not to do, is not to know.
Japanese Proverb

   b) ....

   c) ....

3. What practical steps will you take to positively, i.e., *rationally* impact these myths?

   ....

   ....

   ....

   ....

   ....

   ....

CHAPTER 4

Big Ideas

Big Idea #1: Most organizations and individuals are inherently conservative. We look for and follow others who have already gone down the paths we are walking. We seek security by following their models.

Big Idea #2: The hierarchical organizational structure was adopted from the Catholic church and the Prussian Military in the 18th and 19th centuries as industrial era corporations struggled to find ways of organizing massive growth.

Big Idea #3: Throughout most of the industrial era the soul of many organizations has revolved around the vision and values of the founder or a charismatic leader – just as the Church built on the mythology of Papal infallibility.

What do you do when the leader dies? What do you do when the soul never existed? You create one. You "reverse the phase" and "go boldly where no one has gone before."

CHAPTER 4

Why Can't Corporations Think More Like People?

The will to do springs from the knowledge that we can do.
James Allen

You must first clearly see a thing in your mind before you can do it.
Alex Morrison

Think!
Believe!
Dream!
Dare!
Walt Disney

While their organizational mythology may characterize them as champions of change, most established businesses tend to adopt proven technologies and methods, cautiously avoiding the new and unproved. By their very nature, existing companies are inherently conservative and followers of the well-beaten path.

Inventors of new machines or technology, and the sales people they hire to sell these products, call this the Rule of Seconds: *Nobody wants to be the first to use a new technology. But if it works, everybody wants to be the second.*

The same rule applies to reforging a corporation for more efficiency; nobody really wants to be the first to change things unless the change is modeled on a proven success.

So often we watch company A adopting the methods of company B, who may already be revising their structure to copy Company C's – who are busily trying to find someone else to imitate.

There was a time when corporate models on the scale of today's were virtually non-existent because there weren't many around to emulate. Any 18th century corporate leader looking for successes worth copying encountered no IBM, General Motors or AT &

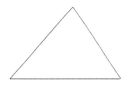

Characteristics of the hierarchical Second Wave, Industrial Organization.
Control Based.
Top Down.
Centralized.
Change Resistant.
Bureaucratic.
Specialized.

T. But they copied anyway. They chose two examples whose management structures not only worked but had been proven effective for centuries: The Catholic Church and the military. Both were classic pyramid structures whose very existence depended upon unflinching top-down discipline.

Of the two, the Church was perhaps more persuasive as a model. After all, *Moses was history's first CEO.* (Wherever there is a manager, a consultant is sure to follow. Those who know their Old Testament will recognize that Jethro, Moses' father-in-law, was the first management consultant. Moses also had perhaps history's first recorded case of executive burnout, and went on the First Strategic Planning Session to an executive retreat in the wilderness, but that's another story . . .)

Isn't the Catholic church *still* the ideal model for the traditional corporation? Doesn't the organization of Pope, Cardinals, Bishops, etc. perfectly parallel the structure of President, Division Vice-President, Area Manager, etc.? And don't pyramidal corporations function on military lines similar to those designed by Augustus Caesar, relying on a direct chain of command from General to private, or from Board Room to Mail Room? And what was the foundational mythology? The infallibility of the Pope.

Many early corporations prospered and thrived on the power of a singular vision. The vision and the values it inspired were almost always established and nurtured by one man who was either a) so driven by greed, avarice and the pursuit of power that he could, to some degree, be certified obsessive or even borderline insane, or b) a leader with such a positive, compelling vision that people were drawn to both the leader and his/her organization as though to a magnet.*

The corporate vision was communicated downward through the pyramidal corporate structure directly from the founder. It was crystallized and unshakable, as though forged from cast iron and mounted on granite. If we choose to, we may see these men (they were invariably men) as stubborn individuals whose business skills would be out of touch with today's methods. But perhaps they weren't. Perhaps among all the serious flaws possessed by such men was a nugget of wisdom and a clarity of vision that is missing from too many contemporary corporations.

It may go by various names, but I suggest it inspired a soul – a corporate soul.

Many of these companies were founded and prospered as a reflection of a singular vision and system of values, only to flounder when those values were altered, ignored or discarded. Interestingly enough, given today's emphasis on service industries, companies whose success depends on provid-

You have to think BIG to be BIG.

Formula for second wave success:
Become a monomaniac with a mission.
P. Drucker

---

*Perhaps Andrew Carnegie was the best example of this type of leader. His professed lifetime goals were: 1) To amass an enormous personal fortune, and 2) To give it all away.

Put all your eggs in one basket and ... watch that basket.

How much was that again?

"How much did you say I have given away, Poynton?" Andrew Carnegie asked his secretary before his death.

"$327 656 399," Poynton replied.

"Good heaven!" Carnegie replied. "Where did I ever get that much money?"

To desire is to obtain; to aspire is to achieve.
            James Allen

The empires of the future are empires of the mind.
        Winston Churchill

You see things; and you say, "Why?" But I dream things that never were; and I say, "Why Not?"
    George Bernard Shaw

ing high levels of service tend to thrive on a reflection of one individual's personality, and suffer when those human values are altered or lost. It is as though a single individual can define the essence of service quality, but an entire organization cannot.

Consider these examples:

Continental Airlines – The direct product of founder Robert Six's imagination (Six was once described as "the last of the old scarf-and-goggles aviators"*), Continental rose from one spindly aircraft flying U.S. Mail routes to a $1 billion corporation. With Six's death and under the aegis of short-term profit seekers, the airline soon stumbled into near-bankruptcy and is only now struggling to emerge. Six personified his airline's success and generated near-legendary levels of employee and customer loyalty – levels that dropped dramatically in the hands of the bean-counters and take-over artists who succeeded him.

Pan American Airlines – Once the most glamorous airline in the world, Pan Am directly reflected the soul and vision of Juan Trippe. Trippe's decision to place the first order for 747s for Pan Am identified that aircraft as the new global standard in intercontinental service. The dramatic decline dates back to 1969, when Trippe gave up his leadership of the firm. With him went the glamorous vision, soon followed by the

*Everybody's Business – The Irreverent Guide to Corporate America (Harper & Row), 1980.

Where there is no vision,
the people perish . . .
        Bible, Proverbs 29:18

No vision and you perish;
No ideal, and you're lost;
Your heart must ever
cherish
Some faith at any cost.
Some hope, some dream
to cling to,
Some rainbow in the sky,
Some melody to sing to,
Some service that is high.
        Harriett Du Autermont

Cherish your visions and
your dreams as they are
the children of your soul;
the blue prints of your ulti-
mate achievements.
        Napoleon Hill

disappearance of one of the airline industry's most revered names.

Leo Burnett Inc. – Advertising agencies are created and dissolved on a turnover schedule that rivals the life-cycle of fruit flies . . . or at least rock bands. But one – Leo Burnett Inc. – has maintained its own name and identity – and much of its soul – for almost 70 years. On the day Leo Burnett opened his office, in the middle of the Great Recession, he placed a bowl of red apples in the reception room as a gesture of welcome and good-will. Then he went out and secured accounts such as Maytag, Hoover and Kellogg. You don't base 70 years of success on a bowl of apples, of course. But their reflection of Burnett's humanistic values said a good deal about the way the company operated. It still operates that way today, as a major international ad agency with billings measured in the hundreds of millions of dollars. And there's still a bowl of red apples in every office reception room.

Would the singular vision and fixed determination of Robert Six, Juan Trippe and Leo Burnett work today? Yes, to a point. It still takes a singular vision to move a corporation in a given direction. (You may have noticed that the world contains darn few statues erected to committees.) From there, it takes teamwork to maintain momentum. But by definition, teams have multiple personalities, multiple ambitions, multiple talents and multiple values. These qualities both define and

Third Wave Organizational Architecture

Characteristics
- *Continuously Improving*
- *Quality Focused*
- *Customer Centered*
- *Totally Participative*

limit teams unless something else is evident – something that unites each member within the team framework, while permitting freedom for all to think and function as individuals.

The difference is a corporate soul.

ACTIVITIES

1. What is the shape of your organizational architecture? Is the customer the centre of all you do?

....
....
....
....
....
....
....
....

2. What is your personal and organizational vision?

....
....
....
....
....
....
....
....
....

CHAPTER 5

Big Ideas

Big Idea #1: Over the past 40 years, Japan has managed a masterful transformation by creatively linking the strengths of a tradition bound hierarchical culture with the transformational power of individuals working in empowered teams.

Big Idea #2: The idea that the Japanese act like automatons is a myth.

Big Idea #3: The idea that no one can compete with the Japanese in the arena of continuous improvement and quality manufacturing is a myth.

Big Idea #4: Excellence knows no national or racial boundaries. Success is based on a strict adherence to truth and reality.

CHAPTER 5

The Maddening Multiple Visions of Japan.

It takes a heart-to-heart unity of purpose of many people if they are to become 'masters' who effectively operate machines and social structures and thus contribute to mankind.

S. Honda

I don't really find it (continuous improvement) very exacting because I am doing what I like to do. As the proverb goes, "Love shortens distance." A person who is trying to invent or contrive something new is enjoying himself although he may appear to others to be having a hard time.

S. Honda

For the past 20 years or so, the driving force behind much of North American corporate thinking has been not the singular vision of a company's leader but the multiple visions of foreign societies.

What we have seen in recent years is the rise of a new business management philosophy – one which I believe has rushed in to fill the vacuum created by the disappearance of that singular shared vision I call the corporate soul. The new business philosophy goes something like this:

> *"Those guys (i.e., offshore competition) are to blame for our troubles. So we'll fix them. We'll copy the things they did to cause us trouble. Then we'll turn their own tools on <u>them</u> and see how they like it!"*

The trouble is, of course, it rarely worked.

Through the 70s and 80s "them" tended to be Japanese corporations, and the reasons grew as familiar as a Sony trademark or a Honda Civic grille. Over two generations, Japan achieved more growth as an industrialized nation than any other country since the Industrial Revolution began. Remember the tendency of established corporations to seek out and emulate models? What could be more compelling as a model than the success of an entire nation of corporations? The success these companies achieved in producing not only new levels of quality in their products but new levels of satisfaction and loyalty among their customers is legendary. You might even say they are mythical.

And therein lies the problem.

The myths of Japanese management prowess are well-known. The most familiar one is probably: *"The Japanese are like automatons. They all perform their duties as they should. That's why they do well in a quality environment."*

This particular myth is reassuring because it supposedly explains the superiority of Japanese corporations in *some* business activities (note the italics) where they out-perform North American corporations engaged in the same activities. It is based on the irrational generalization that Japanese society is much more disciplined than our own. Unfortunately, the myth overlooks some contrasting facts.

The fact is that *effective quality practices are learnable by anyone, at any level of any organization.* Don't just take my word for it – take Einstein's, who said: "What one person can learn almost all people can learn." To suggest that only the Japanese are capable of achieving high levels of quality is wrong and, it seems to me, inherently racist.

The Ties That Bind

The U.S./non-profit organization Corporate Data Exchange discovered, in the early 1980s that:

Effective quality practices are learnable by anyone, at any level of any organization.

If you only care enough for a result, you will almost certainly attain it.
William James

All patterned forms repeat their pattern sequentially.
J. G. Gallimore

Everything is connected to everything else.

A butterfly waves its wings in Japan and three weeks later a tornado strikes Florida.

All motion is cyclic. It circulates to the limits of its possibilities and then returns to its starting point.
Robert Collier

Everything must be challenged in the quest for improvement.

Improvement means a closer approximation of truth, quality, excellence.

- *Pension funds of U.S. Steel and Bethlehem Steel had a total of $133 million invested in ten leading U.S. banks.*
- *The ten banks had loaned $200 million to Japanese steel companies.*
- *The same Japanese steel companies used the loans to develop export markets, targeting the U.S. for cheaper raw steel sales.*
- *The two major U.S. steel companies, unable to compete, began laying off or dismissing outright workers whose pension contributions had financed the end of their own jobs.**

In reality when we look closely we will find that – the Japanese quality/constant improvement process runs contrary to the strict disciplines and traditions of Japanese culture, for it teaches that *everything must be challenged* in the quest for improvement. Interestingly enough, this is a distinctly western (Greek, originally) democratic concept which is clearly at odds with our perception of Japanese society. (And by now, every manager worth his or her expense account knows that the concept was introduced by an American, Edwards Deming, who validated his thesis not in postwar Japan but in Hawthorne, Illinois, during the 1920s and 30s).

Which leads to yet another fact that contradicts the "automaton" stereotype of the Japanese: *Radical empowerment of the workforce.* Does that idea

---

Everybody's Business

sound even vaguely robotic? Hardly. It sounds more like the kind of egalitarian thinking that sprang from the American Revolution, and which has inspired virtually every forward step in social and cultural progress since that time.

But the reality is that two out of three corporations attempting the transformation are doomed to failure. Why do many North American companies have difficulty implementing a concept so closely allied with their own social structure?

No man ever had a new idea while formally dressed.
Sir Frederick Banting

Because they lack the core values, process and structure necessary to adapt their existing facilities. And that's the purpose of this book: To identify the loss represented by the disappearance of core values (the "corporate soul") and generate or at least articulate the process and structure needed to implement ideas that have been around for as long as there has been a human soul.

Empowerment
Isn't it curious that in a democratic society founded on the principles of individual freedom and responsibility that the two locations where they are rarely found are in the home and at work.

The corporate soul of every organization possessing one is both complex and unique. But in my experience all the great ones share, to one extent or another, an appreciation for the rights, the dignity and the contribution of each individual member.

The almost unlimited potential power for change that every individual possesses can and must be harnessed, and a system exists to achieve that goal. I know, because I have introduced it to dozens of corporations, big and small, myth-ridden and (almost) myth-free.

The time to repair the roof is when the sun is shining.
John F. Kennedy

ACTIVITIES

1. Have you and your organization been driven to change and improve by external forces such as foreign competitors?

The wise person avoids evil by anticipating it.
Publilius Syrus

Let our advance worrying become advance thinking and planning.
Winston Churchill

2. What are you currently doing to empower yourself and your colleagues?

------

3. What are you doing to harness the creative potential for change of all your colleagues?

CHAPTER 6

Big Ideas

Big Idea #1: Anyone who fails to study and learn from history is doomed to repeat it.

Big Idea #2: We examine some Facts and Truths about the Japanese economic miracle.

Big Idea #3: We want to understand that the Japanese are not invincible. What they have done is doable by any organization or nation that is prepared to discover and master the principles of success.

CHAPTER 6

Japan – Fact and Fiction.

In assessing the power of individuals to shape an organization as a reflection of a shared corporate soul, let's deal with facts and truths – facts which serve as a background for creating an environment to foster the achievement of corporate goals, and truths which can be applied to any organization bent on achieving success through constant change.

No matter what you believe, it doesn't change the facts.
Al Kersha

We'll begin with some basic facts about Japan:

Facts do not cease to exist because they are ignored.
Aldous Huxley

Fact #1: Japan is exceedingly good at running manufacturing industries and astonishingly bad at organizing other types of businesses.

Few challenges in global industry are more daunting than going head-to-head against firms such as Toyota, Hitachi or Mitsubishi. It seems every aspect of their operations, from product design through manufacturing, marketing to customer follow-up service, functions on a higher plane than reached by the most ambitious and dedicated North American imitators. Japanese dominance in this area is mythical.

Knowledge is of little value until it is . . .
* Gathered
* Communicated
* Applied

Ah, but . . .

A world of difference exists between designing and manufacturing hard goods, and creating and dispensing ideas. And if Alvin Toffler's much-celebrated Third Wave will indeed be knowledge-based, where does that leave "Japan Incorporated"? The impact may already be evident.

One vital aspect of knowledge is the fact that it has no value of its own until it is: a) gathered; b) communicated; and c) applied. The Japanese, and their approach to management principles, have been noticeably ineffective in applying and communicating knowledge on a broad scale. By "broad scale," I include the ability to generate and market something of value based on creativity, intellect and intuition, as opposed to tangible products such as automobiles, VCRs and appliances.

No one acknowledges this with more chagrin – and red ink – than the massive Japanese multinationals who bought into Hollywood dream factories in the late 1980s. By April 1995, Matsushita had sold most of its investment in the U.S. film industry at a loss of several billion dollars. The Japanese apparently were unable to apply their management magic in the weird nether-world of Hollywood dreams and machinations.

The same week that Matsushita took their Hollywood bath, however, the company cut a ribbon on its newest North American investment: a massive expansion of its cellular telephone manufacturing facility in Atlanta, Georgia. Good-bye, mass entertainment. Hello again, mass production.

An idea isn't responsible for the people who believe in it.

Don Marquis

Sony has retained its investment in Columbia Pictures, but only after writing off a $3 billion loss. True, the music division of Sony continues to generate a return on Sony's investment. But it is also true that this division remains the most "hands-off" operation of Sony's entire foreign investment portfolio.

The message, I suggest, is this:

Truth does not change because It Is, or Is not, believed by a majority of the people.

Giordano Bruno

The soul of Japanese industry resides in a number of areas, but Hollywood is not one of them. Successful companies – even brilliantly managed firms like Sony and Matsushita – who betray their corporate soul, or who try to acquire someone else's, are doomed to failure. (For a contrast to the experiences of Sony and Matsushita, see Honda's in Chapter 3.)

Truth #1: To ensure success, ensure that your goals are aligned with your talents and your system of values.

Fact #2: Japan manages to achieve major advances by fostering a sense of freedom in decision-making among one of the

Appearances are deceptive.

Aesop

most disciplined societies in the modern industrialized world.

North American business leaders have marveled for years at the ability of Japan's industrial business leaders to respond quickly to changing markets by modifying their product designs, and sometimes even their basic product concepts.

One might speak to great length of the three corners of reality – what was seen, what was thought to be seen, and what was thought ought to be seen.

Marvin Bell

Would the Sony Walkman have been created if millions of North Americans hadn't developed a passion for jogging? Not likely.

When the U.S. government set targets for automotive fuel economy in the 1970s, Japanese car manufacturers invested time and money to produce cars to meet those standards on schedule; U.S. manufacturers invested similar amounts in hiring Washington lobbyists to protest that the standards were unreasonable.

Dozens more illustrations exist of the Japanese ability to identify social changes and respond to them with products that achieve astonishingly high levels of success. By contrast, many North American companies have appeared fixed, inflexible and sluggish. But here's the conundrum:

We must have strong minds, ready to accept facts as they are . . .

Harry S. Truman

We in the democratic west pride ourselves on being the most free and open societies in the world – arguably the most open in all world history. So why can't our free and open societies generate a business climate possessing the same degree of freedom?

The enigma is doubled when you acknowledge that Japanese society is generally regarded among the world's most closed and restrictive – at least in terms of social mores and interlocking relationships. This is reflected in the powers of the *zaibatsu*, great combines of corporations engaged in favoring member firms to the exclusion of all others. From raw materials to engineering, finance, manufacturing and mar-

Things are more like they are now, than they have ever been before.

Dwight D. Eisenhower

*The facts are always
friendly . . . every bit of
evidence one can ac-
quire, in any area leads
one that much closer to
what is true.*

Carl Rogers

keting, *zaibatsu* members operate in a "scratch my back and I'll scratch yours" environment which would not be tolerated in Western countries. Nor is this a 20th century phenomenon; some *zaibatsus* trace their origins back to the 17th century.

The power of the *zaibatsus* and the interconnections between banks, resource companies, processors, manufacturers and marketers – plus their enduring close ties with government leaders – helped foster the "Japan Incorporated" label. An apt description, perhaps, and an explanation for much of their economic clout. But the *zaibatsus* are essentially economic and trade relationships. No one at the top of a *zaibatsu* sketched the blueprint for a Honda Civic. Or designed the facia for a Toshiba VCR. Or designed the keyboard action of a Yamaha piano.

How do you explain a corporate giant such as Mitsubishi being capable of maintaining and fostering innovation year after year in product after product? And why does this happen within the confines of a society that places a high value on conformity and cultural routines that trace their origins back to Medieval times and beyond?

Something else is happening in Japan. It is an ability to harness the knowledge of everyone closest to the problem, whether the problem is reducing production defects to zero levels or sculpting the body shape of a new Nikon.

*We must learn to tailor our
concepts to fit reality, instead of trying to stuff reality into our concepts.*

*Victor Daniels and
Laurence Horowitz*

Truth #2: Improvements never happen accidentally. They must be systematically nurtured and proactively harvested.

Fact #3: Fifty years ago, Japanese society and industry were so devastated by war that many Western leaders assumed it would not be self-sufficient again before the end of the century. How the Japanese accomplished the most remarkable economic turnaround in history is a mythic tale from which the wise leader will learn much.

Imagine for a moment that you are the Prime Minister of Japan in 1948. Here is what you face in helping your country recover from World War II:*

- 10 million of your citizens are unemployed.

- Almost as many are homeless.

- The industrial base is in ruins.

- The rice crop – the staple of your country's diet – is barely 2/3 of the norm.

- Using the 1935 economy as a base (100), the current economy measures 55.

- An industrial power with a new global vision – the U.S.A. – is taking charge of many economic and political decisions, and their influence cannot be ignored.

Sit down before facts like a child, and be prepared to give up every preconceived notion, follow humbly wherever and to whatever abyss nature leads, or you shall learn nothing.
Thomas H. Huxley

---

*Ibid. (The Finance Minister was Ishabashi Tanzan, former Editor of the *Oriental Economist*, who won the Prime Ministerial seat in 1956).

No authority is higher than reality.

Peter Zarlenga

What do you do? Where do you begin?

If you are wise – as wise as many of Japan's post-war leaders – you examine the negatives on your list and try reversing them to discover what they represent as possible *positive* forces. Turn them around. In the parlance of electronics engineers, *reverse the phase* and see what happens.*

This means deliberately and intentionally breaking with tradition.

It means choosing the road less traveled.

It means fostering freedom of thought within a firm goal-oriented structure.

It means, in a way, reversing the existing phase.

High unemployment? That's a negative. Reverse the phase and treat it as a positive: A massive pool of labor, much of it skilled, to be directed *toward new tasks*.

Heavy industry destroyed? Can't get much more negative than that. Reverse the phase and draw upon a reassuring positive: a natural by-product of all wars is advanced technology. Replace the old industrial plants with new cutting-edge technology, in *a leap ahead*

---

*I was reminded of this phenomenon on a visit to a power generating station located near both a hospital and an adjoining residential area. The power generation process creates a low rumbling sound that could be disturbing to the plant's neighbors - but they never hear it even though the sound continues to exist. Why? Because the plant produces (through electronic amplification) an identical sound, in volume and tone (less than 30 Hz), that is 180 degrees out of phase with the original sound. So the phenomenon continues to exist - but nobody knows it.

of other countries who are reluctant to abandon existing plants no matter how inefficient they may be. Then fill in the gaps where necessary. Or as one cynical Japan-observer put it: "Borrow the best. Invent the rest."

Major loss of government leaders? Move laterally with bold moves such as appointing an economic journalist as Finance Minister. Instruct him to create an Economic Stabilization Board to coordinate production, and a Reconstruction bank to channel capital into selected industries. In other words, *create a fixed infrastructure within which free choices can be made leading toward a common, broadly-based objective.*

For here we are not afraid to follow truth wherever it may lead...
Thomas Jefferson

What's the lesson here? Can it be applied to business organizations as well as it was applied to post-war Japan?

It can. It will again.

Truth #3: Having no wealth and no industry is admittedly a problem. A far greater problem is having no ideas about how to create wealth. As long as you possess ideas, you are able to convert problems to opportunities through the addition of skills and applied intelligence.

ACTIVITIES

1. What is the impact on your soul of this amazing story of Japanese accomplishment?

2. What is the current state of affairs within your organization?

3. How can this story inspire you and your colleagues?

CHAPTER 7

Big Ideas

Big Idea #1: Examples of "reversing the phase" are universal and universally instructive.

Big Idea #2: IBM was once thought to be as unbeatable as Japan Inc. That too was a myth.

CHAPTER 7

The Tale of Two Steves.

We can chart our future clearly and wisely only when we know the path which has led to the present.

Adlai Stevenson

No matter what unforeseen developments in business occur over the next few generations, you can be sure that one case study will appear in every future textbook (in whatever format textbooks may take a few decades hence). The case, of course, is IBM versus Apple. The tale of how Two Steves took on Big Blue. The implications are so complex that, a decade and a half later, analysts and authors continue to mine it for lessons to be learned.

One lesson, reminiscent of those acquired from post-Hiroshima Japan, is provided by Joel Arthur Barker.* He identified four seemingly (remember those dinosaurs?) immutable rules IBM was following on the very day Steve Jobs and Steve Wozniak first swept the floor in that California garage to make room for their careers as computer manufacturers.

Remember that IBM at the time was as dominant in its field as any corporation in history. In the computer market, IBM was the classic 800-pound gorilla that sat wherever it chose to sit. Question IBM's rules for success? You might as well question Newtonian physics.

Here were IBM's four rules:

Life . . . can only be understood backwards. . .

Sören Klerkegaard

---

*Future Edge (William Morrow & Company: New York, 1992)

Rule #1: IBM manufactures their own microprocessors – the heart of their computers – and they are among the best in the world at doing it. So *why should they change?*

Rule #2: IBM retains a very talented software-writing group on staff – again, among the best in the world – and consequently writes all the programs for use exclusively in its own computers. The programs work superbly, they generate immense profits, and they represent valuable corporate assets. *Why change?*

Rule #3: IBM computers are sold only by IBM sales people. Are they among the best-educated, best-trained and best-motivated sales staff in the world? How did you guess? *And why should IBM change?*

Rule #4: Only an IBM technician can open an IBM computer. Permitting the computer to be opened by an unauthorized person may void the warranty. Everyone respects this rule. IBM profits from it. *Again, why change?*

Can we fault IBM for adhering to these guidelines? Hardly. It all made good business sense. More important, the policy generated outstanding success – IBM was the major corporation of its time, incapable (it seemed) of making a bad decision. The corporate structure wasn't broke. So nobody fixed it.

Put yourself in the shoes of the Two Steves facing IBM's dominance, and

When I want to understand what is happening today or try to decide what will happen tomorrow, I look back.

Oliver Wendell Holmes, Jr.

To change the world . . .
one desk at a time.
Reputed to be the
Mission Statement of
Steve Jobs.

You will become as small
as your controlling desire;
or as great as your domi-
nant aspiration.
James Allen

Success has made fail-
ures of many people.

compare their situation with postwar Japan's.

Their positions are similar.

How do you fight the existing situation? You don't. You *change* the existing situation.

How do you face the other side's strengths head-on? You don't. You *develop entirely new strengths*. By starting over. By reversing the phase.

So here come Apple's four *new* rules:

1. Apple can't afford to make its own processors, so *it buys them from other sources*.

2. Apple can't afford to hire software programmers, so *it invites others to write the programs for its product*.

3. Apple has no salespeople and no sales outlets, so *it sells its product through existing stores*.

4. Apple wants as many people as possible to use its computers, so *it makes its products easy to open and modify*. Removing the cover from an Apple computer doesn't negate the warranty; *it leads to a better use of the product*.

This is not a critique, by the way, of IBM. It made no sense at all for the company to change the four rules listed above. *But it made perfect sense for Apple to do so.* Moreover, IBM's ultimate and successful response to Apple, even with its various corporate and product stumbles (Does anyone remember the ill-fated PC Jr.?) is a case study in itself, a remarkable example of a giant company reassessing its position and, like a great ship in the middle of the ocean, eventually turning itself around and sailing back into the mainstream again.

The immutability of IBM was a myth, a fantasy which prevented the company – in spite of all its talents, assets and good intentions – from dealing with the kind of change generated by Wozniak and Jobs. Wozniak and Jobs *succeeded because they didn't believe the myth* and, not believing the myth, *reversed the phase.* They also tapped a spirit in themselves – one that was unsullied by the bumps and bruises of bean-counters pointing to the need for a first-quarter profit.

In hindsight, it's easy to say, "Sure, Apple made the right moves, but it didn't have any choice."

Yes, it did. One choice – voiced in thousands of boardrooms each business day – would have been to follow the well-beaten track of IBM and prolong a myth by asking: "Why should we re-invent the wheel?"

The reason: *"If you reinvent the wheel, you might come up with a wing."*

That's what Apple did by choosing to reverse the phase and go in the opposite direction.

If you reinvent the wheel you might create a wing.
John Lawrence
Reynolds.

An Apocryphal Tale That's Probably True:

Four senior executives of giant corporations were having drinks at a golf club following a weekend match. When the topic of business came up, one man shook his head. "Don't know how you fellows are handling things," he said, "but we managed to downsize by about 5000 people in the past six months." "Know what you mean," added the second executive. "We lopped almost 10 000 from our staff." He smiled. "Much leaner now." "You guys are pikers," the third man said. "I've spent the last month or so getting rid of about as many people as both of you put together." He grinned. "We're running lean and mean." All three turned to the fourth man, whose expression was glum. "You thinking about how much fat you have to trim?" one of them said to him. "No," the man said, shaking his head sadly. "I've just been listening to you three boast about laying off 30 000 of my customers!"

Once the choice is made and the options remain open, beneficial change can begin *if there is a soul functioning within the body.* In countries (see Japan c. 1948). In computers (see Apple c. 1979). And in companies (see your own, right now, and identify the areas where change is essential).

One more computer story that is neither myth nor fable:

The last I heard, the vast majority of Microsoft employees who have been with the company seven years or more and who exercised their stock options are millionaires. Many are multi-millionaires, capable of living virtually any lifestyle they choose for the rest of their lives without working another day.

So why do they remain employed at Microsoft, in demanding, high-stress positions long after the major growth

It is not something I must do, but something I want to do. . .

James Fixx

cycle of their shareholdings has passed? Are they that greedy? Probably not. Are they "baby-sitting" their assets by showing up every day? Highly unlikely. They are there because they choose to be there. Because they share the vision. Because their jobs are fun and challenging. Because they consider themselves to be integral parts of a corporate soul.

This is not a case of employees staying on the job to satisfy their bodies. It's an excellent illustration of the benefits to be accrued by satisfying their souls.

Help people become more motivated by guiding them to the source of their own power.
Paul Thomas

You cannot teach a person anything. You can only help him discover himself.
Galileo

ACTIVITIES

1. What are the written or unwritten rules or "silent assumptions" within your organization?

....

....

....

....

....

....

....

2. Are these rules exclusive or inclusive? Do they invite people to examine or challenge them?

....

....

....

....

The art of teaching is the art of assisting discovery.
Mark Van Doren

3. What vulnerabilities and strengths do these rules provide to your organization?

CHAPTER 8

Big Ideas

"He who has a why to live can bear with almost any how."
Viktor Frankl

Big Idea #1: The creation of a soul begins by answering the question . . .

Who am I?

Big Idea #2: Who I am (soul/identity) should always direct and empower my behavior (body).

Big Idea #3: Actions speak louder than words. What you do and how you do it is a far more convincing representation of your values than what you say.

Big Idea #4: Seek a healthy balance.

CHAPTER 8

The Why to Live

Three of life's most important questions:
1. Who am I?
2. What do I do?
3. How do I do it?

In early 1996, Pepsico International, the second-largest marketer of cola-based soft drinks in the world, announced a major marketing objective. The company, whose corporate colors had once been red and blue, would strive to be identified henceforth by one color only: Blue.

The announcement did not make reference to its major competitor, world-leader Coca-Cola, whose identity was allied with the color red, but that was unnecessary. Pepsi was ceding Coke's claim to red and seizing blue as its hue.

Many of the stories generated by Pepsi's PR machine were accompanied by a photo of a leased Concorde supersonic jetliner painted in Pepsi's corporate blue colors. It was just another part of the soft drink company's "We're blue!" corporate identity campaign. All the stories mentioned the firms' global budget for the changeover: $500 million in U.S. funds.

Think of that: Half a billion dollars to change the public's perception of the corporate color for a manufacturer of sweetened carbonated water. No doubt the amount can be rationalized by marketing experts as a justifiable expenditure. Cementing your position vis-à-vis your major competitor on a global scale is a major achievement, worthy of substantial investment and extensive commitment of corporate assets. (Marketing people talk like that, especially when pitching for approval of a campaign.)

But $500 million? To change the corporate color I.D. of a soft drink?

I don't question the marketing wisdom of establishing a clear corporate identity for a global company, and I have been known to enjoy the pleasures of a cold cola drink on a hot summer's day. If the move to blue convinces a million people to choose Pepsi over Coke, I assume within a few years Pepsico and its bottlers will have earned back their investment.

But I ask a question that many of you may be asking – a question for which there is no immediate, obvious answer:

Everything can be taken from a person but one thing: the last of the human freedoms – to choose one's attitude in any given set of circumstances, to choose one's own way.

Viktor E. Frankl

What else could have been done with that $500 million? How else could the company have benefited from the expenditure and, in so doing, benefited others? And what are the values of a company that places such a high price on its corporate color?

The answers are less important than the reason for the question. Pepsico has one over-riding goal, no doubt: To displace Coca-Cola – to some degree at least – in consumer share-of-mind and ultimately in sales. The objective of Pepsi's half-billion-dollar budget is not to improve product quality or even expand Pepsi's overall share of the market. Its goal, by its very nature, is crystal-clear. It is an attack on its formidable

The greatest discovery of my generation is that human beings can alter their lives by altering their attitudes of mind.
William James

enemy. It is battlefield strategy. It is a major move in an ongoing market war that, every day of every year, drains substantial quantities of major talents, high intelligence and formidable energy from gifted minds in Pepsi's marketing departments and advertising agencies.

To sell colored water.

The Question That Clinched The Deal

When Apple Computer co-founder Steve Wozniak approached John Scully – then a senior executive with Pepsico Inc. – about assuming the presidency of Apple, Scully at first demurred. "I have a solid career path here," Scully explained. "My future is really with Pepsico."

"What do you want to be known for when you're gone," Wozniak asked. "A guy who helped change the world with new technology? Or a guy who spent his life selling colored water?" Scully took the job at Apple.

Around the time that the Pepsi Blue story broke, another news story reported that retired U.S. General Norman Schwarzkopf earns $75 000 per appearance to lecture business leaders on the idea of thinking like battlefield commanders. Clearly, General Schwarzkopf possesses all the credentials needed to discuss battlefield strategy with whomever he chooses. What's more, he and his agents have the right to charge whatever the market will bear for the man to draw parallels between business competitors and Saddam Hussein.

My problem is that the General is telling his audiences how to fight not only the wrong war, but an unnecessary one. Business histories are overflowing with stories of military masterminds who, upon retirement, turned their leadership talents to running a business and failed miserably. Why? *Because few comparisons are as out of touch with reality as those that equate managing a corporation with directing a battalion in the field.* It is a concept that works only in the narrow minds of unimaginative people whose perceptions are unable to creep past the zero-sum concept of competition which declares: "If I win, you must lose; if I win, you are defeated. If I am the victor with the spoils, you are the loser in the ruins. If I live, you die!"

Let's not forget what happens to your staff in a real all-out war battlefield setting. If they fail, they're likely to die at the hands of their enemy. If they refuse to carry out orders, they are likely to be shot on the command of their superiors. When the war is over and no battles remain to be fought, the survivors will return home with great relief, nursing their wounds, prepared for the effects of delayed shell-shock, and probably determined to avoid the horrors of war for the rest of their lives.

Business is not war. When business becomes as deadly as war in any fashion beyond the stretched-to-excess parallels of the good General, we are all doomed. Just as we will be if the day arrives when war becomes as intrinsic in our lives as business is today.

The World According to Revlon

"In terms of marketing, you've got to have the will to win. You've got to see the blood running down the street. You've got to be able to take it. You've got to be able to shove it. If you're not, you're nobody. You never will be."

Charles Revson, President, Revlon Inc.

ACTIVITIES

1. Who are you? What are your core values and beliefs?

....

....

....

....

....

2. What do you do? What contribution/value do you add?

....

....

....

....

3. How do you do it? In what ways do you expand the pie?

....

....

....

....

CHAPTER 9

Big Ideas

Big Idea #1: There is a "Better Way."

Big Idea #2: It is possible to succeed in the toughest, most demanding areas of business by adopting a creative rather than a negatively competitive market strategy.

Big Idea #3: At the end of the day we will have expended the same amount of energy. The choice is ours – to compete for a greater slice of a finite pie by beating others or to add value, be creative and create a larger pie.

CHAPTER 9

A Better Idea.

One of the world's most successful companies is based not upon a concept of waging war but on a vision of improving the state of humanity. This value may not be inscribed in its corporate doctrine, but it has been at the heart of the firm since its founder began bolting small engines to bicycles shortly after the end of World War Two.

Soijiro Honda was neither a "tree-hugger" nor a corporate softy – you don't build a one-man operation into one of the world's leading automotive corporations in your lifetime by being either. He had inner strength, ambition, perception and a powerful ego driving him to success. He also possessed, in my opinion, two qualities which tend to be at the heart of all successful companies: 1) A deep appreciation for knowledge and 2) A vision extending well beyond his firm's bottom line and his personal life span.

His appreciation for knowledge grew from his training as an engineer. Honda understood the value of innovative engineering and perceptive knowledge, and his firm soon became known for the large proportion of engineers on its staff – larger than any of its competitors. Honda's engineering staff was deemed its most valuable asset, at a time when General Motors reportedly employed more stylists and marketers – and paid them more money – than engineers.

Styling and marketing represents fashion, and fashion by its nature changes. But engineering represents knowledge and skill, and the value of these two assets increases steadily with time when nurtured in a suitable environment.

This is not to say that Honda's marketing skills are second rate. In fact, they are legion. The secret of Honda's marketing successes is that they grew organically out of engineering achievements, instead of vice-versa. *Engineering breakthroughs inspired advances directed towards marketing opportunities, and marketing successes were built upon meeting an existing customer need left unfilled by others.*

No better example exists of this success than Honda's virtual revolution of the motorcycle industry.

Back in the late 1960s, motorcycles were not for the faint of heart. Companies such as Harley-Davidson, Triumph, Norton and BSA reveled in the macho image of their products. Their very sound and appearance were designed to match characteristics of their primary buyers: Aggressive, noisy, uncomfortable, heavy and inefficient.

Yet none of the manufacturers was really prospering or expanding as they might.

The problem was rooted in the severe limitation of buyers who might choose to be identified with a biker's lifestyle. The pleasures of the open road astride a powerful two-wheeled vehicle might be tempting to everyone. But the company you tended to keep was a major deterrent.

Honda knew that motorcycles could be much more refined than those pouring off the Harley-Davidson assembly line. He led his engineers to design a motorcycle that would be comfortable to ride, easy to handle, and more miserly with fuel. The leather-clad bikers sneered at the result, but that didn't matter. Honda wasn't making a product for them; he was offering a new lifestyle to an entirely untouched group of buyers. Instead of directly challenging the competition for one fixed battlefield area, Honda expanded the "battlefield"/market, making more room for everyone.

Suddenly, you didn't have to sacrifice your kidneys to the jolting of a massive cycle in order to enjoy riding with the wind in your face and bugs in your teeth. Didn't have to grow a beard, acquire a tattoo and refer to your spouse as your "old lady" either. You could ride in comfort and in near-silence on a Honda.

And here's where marketing took the lead of engineering, with the brilliant tag-line to Honda motorcycle advertising: *You meet the nicest people on a Honda.*

Soon other Japanese followed the lead. Harley-Davidson sales shrank, and the company almost went under, surviving only by drastically improv-

The art of progress is to preserve order amid change and preserve change amid order.
Alfred North Whitehead

ing its quality level to bring it close to those of Honda.

After establishing itself as a major factor in automotive design, Honda moved into Formula One racing for the same reason – not for what it might win, *but for what it would learn.* The demands on engine and suspension design generated by Formula One racing are awesome. Honda – alone among Japanese car manufacturers – dipped in and out of Formula One competition as its engineers decreed, not as its marketing department dictated. The company's sole purpose was to test new engineering concepts and apply the lessons to its consumer products.

Honda's outstanding success in Formula One racing rarely appeared in its advertising and promotion activities. We saw no Accords with racing stripes in the company's TV commercials. Honda didn't make its investment in Formula One to win awards; it made the investment to acquire knowledge. And that's a key difference.

"They're Running Fins This Year!"

In the 1950s, the most secretive departments of North American auto companies wasn't Engineering; it was Styling. Ford's 15 design studios had locks that could be changed in half an hour. Twenty guards supervised by an ex-FBI agent checked every employee's badge regularly to prevent anyone from being in an area of styling without authorization (chrome trim could not see wheel designs, for example).

Outside, a Security Patrol used a 60-power telescope to watch a nearby grain elevator in case rival spies were on the structure spying in turn on Ford. In spite of this, all the companies always learned the styling secrets of the others.*

In the last ten years of his life, Mr. Honda concentrated his personal attention on the ability of small, efficient and reliable gas engines to provide power where needed. In doing so, he returned to the roots of his company's soul.

Much of the world was (and still is) under-developed. The Third World has little need for large automobiles or even powerful motorbikes. But it has an abiding need for dependable electric power, especially in clinics, hospitals and schools. That's where Honda focused the same engineering talents he first brought to bear on motorbikes. As a result, in almost every country in the world you'll often find a small Honda gas-powered generator supplying power to light schools . . . operate hospital equipment . . . and generally improve the quality of many more lives than any single gas-powered vehicle could hope to achieve. To me, this demonstrates the presence of a soul in the organization – one that values both the bottom line and its impact on society.

Best of all, Honda's firm has managed to grow not by dominating the battlefield, but by expanding it . . . and

---

* *Everybody's Business*

not by targeting new markets but by
building on existing knowledge.

ACTIVITIES

1. To which model – creative or competitive – are you and your organization committed?

2. Make a list of things you could do
   to be more creative.

.

CHAPTER 10

Big Ideas

Big Idea #1: We all wear blinkers that focus, direct and restrict our vision and openness to possibilities. Every organization has them too.

Big Idea #2: The true test of one's values is: "What do you do with your limited resources?"

Big Idea #3: Do we work for money or spiraré?

CHAPTER 10

Blinkers or Spiraré?

*Recall the Tires? Hell, No, Just Call Jimmy's Agent!**

In October 1977, Firestone was accused of knowingly selling ten million faulty Firestone 500 steel-belted radial tires. At first the company blamed 27 deaths relating to failure of the tires on poor owner maintenance and negative press. When that failed, they launched a major TV campaign featuring movie star Jimmy Stewart in its TV commercials, assuring car owners that the company maintained the same dedication to quality as founder Harvey Firestone had established. The campaign didn't work. Finally, they recalled the tires. Firestone never fully recovered, and was soon purchased by Bridgestone, a Japanese-owned competitor.

Are we born with blinkers, obscuring our vision and limiting our perception? Or do we put them on according to our environment – like wearing galoshes when it snows?

Too often it is the latter occasion that stimulates us to become selectively blind – and the blindness, I suggest, is a direct result of corporate or cultural environments which have either discarded or failed to nurture their soul.

A popular communication exercise illustrates what I mean:

Seven Cynical Steps to Avoid Losing Your Job in the 90s:

1. *Don't work in communications.*

Everybody thinks they can write. Everybody thinks writing and advertising is play. Everybody thinks their spouse knows a good ad or press release when he/she sees it. So if you work in communications, you are expendable.

2. *Always seek approval.*

You were not hired for your creative ideas. You were hired to execute your boss's ideas. If a company wants ideas, it hires a consultant. So if you want to keep your job, keep your ideas to yourself.

3. *Know the difference between an employee and a consultant.*

A consultant must have one good idea an hour. An employee who has more than one good idea a month is considered unstable.

4. *Accept boredom with grace.*

Shorter corporate meetings could threaten someone's job.

5. *Be careful who you trust.*

The higher you go in a company, the more closely you're being watched. Don't be shocked when your loyal subordinates are more loyal to your boss than to you.

(cont. next page)

A group facilitator gathers several volunteers in a furnished room – perhaps a typical living room, crowded with various objects, paintings, accessories and so on. The facilitator tells everyone they are to take two minutes to study the room completely, noting everything in it which is *blue*. At the end of the two minutes, he asks everyone to sit down . . . close their eyes . . . and count all the items in the room which are *red*.

The command, of course, is met with groans from the volunteers. Hey, they were told to pay attention only to blue objects. Who the heck made a point of noticing red things? It's maddening . . . confining . . . and unfair.

Yet isn't this the way many employees are instructed to do their jobs? When we limit our vision to the next quarterly profit statement and eliminate any element of soul that says "You are more than a mere cog in this money-making machine," aren't we equipping people with blinkers, blinding them to opportunities?

The values held by a company's management group have a profound influence on the employees and, it follows, on the very nature of the company's operations. We have all seen (and many of us have worked for) companies whose stated system of values bears little or no relationship to those of its executives. In the parlance of management training consultants, they don't "walk the talk."

6. *Remember: Your boss is never crazy.*
The more bizarre the behavior and the more senior the erratic executive, the more likely his behavior will be excused as evidence of a dynamic visionary under a lot of stress – possibly because he is surrounded by incompetents.

7. *Don't get too comfortable if you are a woman, a visible minority, or gay.*
You may just be filling a quota.

When you encounter a company like that, you can be assured that any goals it sets and any philosophy it follows will be at best ineffective and at worst destructive to morale.

The fact is, employees judge the values of a company, as expressed through its management group, not by what is said but by what is *done*. This represents more than that corny old adage of actions speaking louder than words. In this case, it makes the words themselves meaningless, except to measure the size of the contradictions expressed by leadership's actions.

You can try this experiment for yourself, but I suggest your own perception will produce the answer:

Instead of asking someone – a friend or a colleague – what their values are, watch what they do with their limited resources. Think especially of their limited leisure time. Do they spend it with their children? Do they fill the hours with work? Do they engage in purely social activity, or do they find things to do that refresh the spirit and tone up the body? That's the measure of their true values.

I was reminded of this in the days immediately following the end of the O.J. Simpson trial. We don't have to share our views of that particular event on these pages, but something that happened when the trial finally ended revealed much about Simpson's values – as much as any evidence submitted in court.

Within a few days – *less than a week* – of his acquittal, and following a period of incarceration lasting more than a year, Simpson traveled to Florida for a golfing vacation. All right, a golfer locked away for 15 months or so has a right to all the fresh air and exercise he can seize when finally released. *But this particular day was Simpson's daughter's birthday* – and everyone who learned where Simpson was and what he was doing that day nodded knowingly.

A man separated from his daughter for almost 500 days goes golfing on the other side of the country on her birthday – that's how he chose to spend that particular bit of leisure time.

Nothing he can ever say about his values will speak louder than that choice and that action.

Earlier I mentioned the power of myths. At the time, I referred primarily to negative corporate myths – the reasons and rationalizations for companies not moving forward and embracing positive change. The danger of myths is that they are inherently powerful, and they are powerful because they tend to be based on widely-shared perceptions.

These lead naturally to self-fulfilling prophecies. "We don't do things that way here" is a popular one. Of course we don't do things that way – *because people keep saying we don't!*

I've discovered, however, that corporations whose values are deeply entrenched and literally intrusive in the actions of their employees create their own positive myths. For the sake of clarity, let's call them "spiritual beliefs." In case this term makes some people uncomfortable, perhaps I should point out the origin of the word is from the Latin *Spirare*: *"To breathe, to give life."* That same root is the basis of "inspire" – when you inspire something (or someone), you give them breath and life. Anyone who accepts the risk of launching a business is inspired to take that first step . . . and the corporate spirit rests within that original inspiration.

Spiritual beliefs in corporations are by definition long-term in outlook. Unless you're a youngster opening a lemonade stand for a summer weekend, the spiritual beliefs behind any enterprise must have their sights on the distant horizon.

"Aha," I sense someone thinking. "Sure they're inspired – inspired to make money. Isn't that the basis of every entrepreneur, every business person who signs papers of incorporation?"

ON THE PURPOSE OF LIFE
To Live,
To Love,
To Learn
To Leave A Legacy.
Stephen Covey and
Merrill Douglas

I submit it is not. There are people, of course, who seek only to maximize short-term profits. They're known by many names, few of them flattering. They speculate in land, practicing short-term "flips" of property, or perhaps they corner commodity markets. Whatever their methods, they function primarily as "lone wolves" or "sharks," dependent on few resources except their own daring, perception and financial resources.

Individuals are inspired to launch businesses not by short-term monetary rewards but by long-term vision, inspiration growth, expansion, development and – most crucial of all – a sense of fulfilling a critical need among a large segment of their fellow citizens.

At the root of every decision made by every 20th-century business person is that same need to satisfy an essentially spiritual drive. And present within the philosophy of every successful corporation is a core belief or system of beliefs which qualify, within any definition you may choose, as spiritual values. They may be articulated (with varying levels of clarity) in a Corporate Mission Statement or more sensed than spoken among the majority of the firm's employees.

But corporate spiritual beliefs exist. And their values are rooted on the far horizon, not in the results of the next quarterly statement.

ACTIVITIES

1. List the three organizations you consider to be most successful. Are they motivated by money or spiraré?

....

....

....

....

....

....

2. What do you think are the spiritual values of these organizations?

3. What spiritual values motivate you?

CHAPTER 11

Big Ideas

Big Idea #1: The challenge facing most organizations today is not essentially financial but spiritual in nature.

Big Idea #2: One key characteristic of the soulless organization is the predominance of a "short term" focus.

Big Idea #3: The evidence is in . . . the focus on values pays.

CHAPTER 11

Working on the Wrong Problem.

Success is a by-product of meaningful, purposeful activity.

The Life Cycle of an Organization

1. An idea becomes a movement.
2. The movement becomes an organization.
3. The organization becomes an institution and therein lies the death of the idea.

To every action there is always opposed an equal reaction . . .
Sir Isaac Newton

There are no . . . great gains without some losses, no goods without some evils, no winning without some failing.
David Seaburg

It's my sincere belief that many of our corporations are working on the wrong problem – or at least on problems which are more effect than cause. The core challenge for companies in the 21st century is not an economic one – it is a spiritual one. Corporations in trouble today can trace their origins to the point in their history when they were either unable to renew or unable to sustain the spirit (breath of life) that propelled it to success in the first place.

The results manifest themselves in many ways and with many effects, but none more prevalent and odious than the tyranny of quarterly profit reports. No one has ever launched a new company solely on the basis of turning an acceptable profit in the first quarter. (The vast majority of new business ventures, of course, rarely turn a profit in their first year.) Anyone who insists on showing a profit each quarter on schedule should never venture into business in the first place; they should put their money in term deposits or secure mortgages and do nothing except count their dividends. (An interesting point when you look at the power of pension funds in the stock market today.).

The quarterly profit report should be viewed the same way as an airline pilot may view an altimeter; it shows your craft's vertical movement, but not necessarily your forward progress. Corporations need both short-term results and long-term visions. To ignore one at the expense of the other is to court disaster.

The problems of an exclusively short-term focus are many but the risks are predictable. They include a disastrous drop in employee morale with a corresponding reduction in efficiency and customer service quality. When people are insecure about their jobs and their future – regardless of their own dedication and talents, based on the whims of bean-counters who are as familiar with the prevailing corporate spirit as they are with the mountains of Java – they find it difficult to focus on tasks that involve sincere respect.

Consider the case of K-Mart, in a fight to stay alive in spite of its substantial assets, including name recognition, locations and buying clout. A few years ago, K-Mart executives launched a strategy to improve its profit position. This consisted of reducing overhead by stripping sales-staff levels; making room for younger management personnel who would directly reflect the tastes of the store's core shoppers (the 18-36 age group); and emphasizing service by insisting that all staff close each transaction by mouthing the words, "Thank you for shopping K-Mart!"

I have no idea where this strategy originated, but I can assure you it was not in the mind of anyone who understands and appreciates either the con-

Did you think you could have the good without the evil? Did you think you could have the joy without the sorrow?
David Grayson

Sin, as a saint explained, consists of turning away from eternal things to things merely temporal.
James Salter

The optimist sees the donut, the pessimist, the hole.
McLandburgh Wilson

An optimist sees an opportunity in every calamity; a pessimist sees a calamity in every opportunity.
Winston Churchill

cept of corporate spirituality or the essence of human nature.

First, releasing store managers on the basis of "bringing younger talent up" is a bean-counter strategy. Every corporation needs rejuvenation, but it should be based solely on merit, not on an arbitrary age cut-off. When K-Mart released large numbers of its store and department managers with 20 or more years of experience, it might as well have moved half its prime store locations to rural Montana in terms of clever use of its corporate assets. The knowledge and experience of those people was as valuable an asset to the company as any real estate on the books. By replacing them with younger, less experienced staff it may have gained a fresh insight into the tastes of its audience – although no definitive proof seems to exist – but it pushed insight, ability and an embodiment of whatever corporate spirit still existed out the back door. It also, by the way, launched a series of expensive and pesky wrongful dismissal suits, which lofted the spirits of the firm's lawyers and further deflated the morale of long-term employees.

At the customer service level the results were even more devastating. K-Mart employees saw their benefits slashed and their work-load increased dramatically. They saw long-term managers to whom they owed their first loyalties disappear and were told, in so many words: "Produce or else!"

Oh yes. And they were instructed to smile at every shopper and say, "Thank You for Shopping K-Mart." With deep sincerity of course.*

This is like asking a fish to swim and fly at the same time. Yet K-Mart management were amazed when their strategy failed miserably. Consider the paradox: Massive downsizing, threatening, firing, cutting benefits, etc. while insisting that employees smile and say "Thank you for shopping K-Mart!" Who's kidding whom here??

By early 1996, the results of K-Mart's efforts were so devastating that the chain was rumored to be looking for a buyer. When no suitors appeared, management announced it had no choice but to begin closing some store locations, throwing more employees out of work. Naturally, blame was placed in a number of areas, including high overhead, strong competition and shrinkage of the overall retail market. So those employees who followed the rules – who gave up benefits, accepted cuts in their income, assumed added responsibilities and saw competent managers dismissed on the basis of seeking a younger point-of-view – now faced the prospect of losing their jobs anyway.

This is a superb example of the philosophy which says, "I screwed up, so

A human being without a set of values would likely lead a dismal and destructive life. A corporation without a set of values would likely be a dismal and depressing place to work.
Will Barrett, Executive Vice-President, AVCO Financial Services Ltd.

---

*I am told that in some stores customers were confused when K-Mart staff would bid them good-bye by saying "TYFSKM" – pronounced "Tiff Skim." Shoppers who asked what it meant were informed that it stood for "Thank You for Shopping K-Mart," but that the harried staff didn't have time to say the entire phrase.

you have to pay." I have no idea what became of the executives who instigated the "Get tough and make 'em smile" philosophy. But if they lost their jobs I would guess that they had wider, softer and more golden parachutes than any retail staff possessed.

On a vastly more positive note . . . it's difficult to discuss something that is spiritual without touching on the question of ethics. I do not believe that ethical standards and successful business management are exclusive to each other, nor have they ever been. But there are degrees of ethical behavior, and those firms which operate according to the highest ethical standards have, in my opinion, the strongest corporate spiritual presence. What's more, both the presence and the resulting standards lead to direct benefits. Here's proof:

During the 1980s groups of investors in Canada and the U.S. began looking beyond quarterly bottom-line performance of targeted companies, focusing on other aspects of their operation. These included not only the way in which the company treats its employees and suppliers, but also the kinds of business it engages in and the countries in which it operates. Soon these investor values were reflected in mutual fund companies created to pursue them with "ethical" portfolios. By filtering out companies which engage in unfair business practices or produce repellent products, selective investors

All achievement, all earned riches, have their beginning in an idea.
Napoleon Hill

could satisfy both their income needs and their conscience.

Typical of the standards set by mutual fund managers are those established by Ethical Funds of Vancouver:

- Demonstrate progressive industrial relation practices.
- Conduct business only in countries practicing racial equality.
- Avoid discrimination by sex, age, race or similar characteristics.
- Live up to environmental responsibilities.
- Do not produce goods or services directly related to tobacco, military products or nuclear power.

Behind these ethical values was more than conscientious behavior. Investors assumed, for example, that companies practicing progressive industrial relations would attract higher-quality employees and suffer fewer work stoppages due to strikes and other unrest. The result could only be a positive impact on the bottom line. Similarly, firms living up to their environmental responsibilities would pay fewer fines and not suffer the drawbacks of poor public relations.

When ethical investing began, traditional investors laughed and assumed that anyone purchasing shares of an ethically-based mutual fund must be more interested in hugging trees than reaping profits.

As it turns out the laugh is on them; ethically-based mutual funds have

Long-range planning does not deal with future decisions, but with the future of present decisions.
Peter Drucker

tended to perform in the top half of their category year after year.

ACTIVITIES

1. What percentage of your time and creativity do you invest in long term vs. short term focused activities?

_____

_____

_____

_____

_____

_____

_____

_____

2. What steps will you take to strike a more healthy balance?

_____

_____

_____

_____

_____

_____

_____

_____

_____

_____

CHAPTER 12

Big Ideas

Big Idea #1: Any organization lacking a "soul" will be ineffective at change management.

Big Idea #2: The successful 21st century organization must be customer-centred and a hierarchical architecture will doom it to failure.

Big Idea #3: The "Better Way" to customer-centredness, empowerment, ownership and continuous improvement.

CHAPTER 12

Changing the Shape of the Organization

TOWARDS A NEW LANGUAGE . . . FOR A CHANGE.*

The Wall Street Journal recently identified ten descriptions of ways that North American corporations are attempting to foster change. They are:

1. **Thinking Out of the Box:** *Creating new processes, not just tinkering with old formulae.*
2. **In Alignment:** *Emphasizing employees whose values and attitudes are compatible with those of the boss. (See #1 – Is there a conflict here?)*
3. **Empowerment:** *Pushing decisions as far down as possible.*
4. **Constant Whitewater:** *Being able to manage in an age of mergers, cutbacks and re-engineering.*
5. **Face Time:** *Equating time spent in the office with real success.*
6. **Disconnect:** *A breakdown in communication; a mild term for disagreement. Which can lead to . . .*
7. **Derailment:** *Getting kicked off the fast track due to a disconnection or a deficiency in skills or style.*

(cont. on the next page)

"What," I hear a CEO saying now (and I see his or her gaze: cool, steely, quietly demanding), "can adding a spirit, a soul, whatever you want to call it, do for our organization beyond making us feel good? What can it do about customer service? What can it do about making a positive effect on all the kinds of hard-nosed decisions that I have to make every day?"

In a word, everything.

Let's deal with change first.

Bodies – yours, mine and your organization's – adapt to change very slowly. In fact, from generation to generation, the environment around us changes faster than the bodies of creatures existing within that environment. Think of those dinosaurs whose bones I viewed in Alberta. Or think of this:

Imagine decreasing the level of oxygen in the air we breathe by 1/10th of one percent every hundred years. Assuming nothing else changes in our environment, that would produce a ten percent reduction in oxygen levels after 10 000 years, compared with today's. It's pretty clear to me – and to biologists – that human beings and most other animal life would adapt to this change little by little over the years until, 10 000 years hence, they would still be functioning as well as you and I do now, with ten percent less oxygen to breathe.

8. **Delayering:** The "smart bomb" version of a cutback. Instead of a blanket layoff, companies may select one layer of management – usually the middle – and eliminate it all together. (Also known as "flattening the structure.")

9. **Core Competencies:** Generalists in a management position who see "the big picture".

10. **In Transition:** An unemployed executive

REPORT ON BUSINESS - August 8th, 1995

Compared with us their lungs, muscles and entire body would be functioning at much higher levels of efficiency than ours – able to produce the same level of energy on ten percent less oxygen.

But plunk yourself down right now in an atmosphere containing ten percent less oxygen than we have been accustomed to, and you will suffer noticeably. Depending on your current physical state, you would likely survive, but your energy level would be curtailed considerably and you would suffer the effects of oxygen deprivation such as headaches and nausea.

In effect, your descendants 10 000 years hence would have the luxury of time to adapt to the changed environment but you wouldn't, and you would pay the price as a result.

Now think in terms of your corporate "bricks and mortar" as the physical body of your operation – which, of course, it is. Let's suppose your company includes a vast array of equipment for manufacturing, processing, handling, distribution, etc., and imagine that a technological change arrives tomorrow which will cut your operating expenses significantly if you change all your equipment operation from electric power to hydraulic power. No doubt about it – every-thing will work just as smoothly and for much longer, but at 20 percent less cost. Of course, you'll need to convert every machine on the production line and every peripheral connected to it.

**WILL FUTURE RÉSUMÉS IN-
CLUDE A SENSE OF
HUMOR QUOTIENT?**

By continuously altering
their responses to chang-
ing customer tastes,
many firms are also reas-
sessing the qualities they
most value in their em-
ployees.

At Intel Corp., for exam-
ple, there are no job de-
scriptions anymore. In-
stead, people speak of
"owning" problems or op-
portunities. It's an at-
tempt to deal with con-
stant change. "We
haven't faced a chal-
lenge this big since the Industrial Revolution," said
one Intel executive.

Other firms place high
value on an employee's
desire to do the work.
New CNN employees are
chosen in part for their
ability to deal with ex-
traordinary ambiguity,
while Southwest Airlines
looks for workers with a
sense of humor.

"Can't do it," you'd say. "Not overnight – too much capital cost, too much
disruption, blah, blah, blah."

That's the challenge of changing
physical assets alone. It's like asking
your body to become as efficient on less
oxygen virtually overnight.

But suppose you had to switch
quickly from Imperial to Metric systems . . . or from a 5 day, 8-hour work
week to a 4 day, 10-hour schedule . . .
could your staff do it quickly and effi-
ciently?

If they see themselves as so many
pieces of production equipment,
driven to full capacity and easily re-
placeable with little notice, they will
have difficulty adjusting. They may attempt to adjust out of fear or self-sur-
vival. But the change won't happen
easily or smoothly.

But if your organization has soul – a
sense of shared values and beliefs that
deals with the corporate philosophical
question "Why are we here?", assuming the corporation ever gets around to
asking it – the transition will be much
easier.

Or, to quote *Gernon's First Law of
Soulful Change*:

"A soul in a safe environment is the
most adaptable, change friendly organ-
ism imaginable. Assuming it does not
feel threatened, or that actions don't
seriously challenge its core beliefs, a
corporate soul adapts to change more
easily, more smoothly and less defen-

sively than any other aspect of the organization."

At the risk of sounding more ecclesiastical than I intend to, look at it this way:

The "bricks and mortar" assets of your corporation – everything that does not go home when you close down for the day – are transitory or situational; the soul or shared spirit of your company is permanent and abiding.

This leads to *Gernon's Second Law of Soulful Change*:

"Faced with an unstable situation, managers tend to hold on to those aspects of their work which appear to be fixed and immutable – such as the organizational structure – but which are in fact transitory and situational."

This is the most difficult barrier to surmount in corporate change. It is the primary reason why, logical and persuasive as the case may be for change, it is resisted at various levels within the company.

I'll bet you've encountered crises in your day relating to an entire litany of challenges relating to constant change, including:

• Loss of market or declining market share.

• Erosion of customer base and loyalty.

• Effects of technological change on a massive scale.

• Rise of new competition.

- Unanticipated changes in fashion, taste, social mores, etc.
- Loss of competitive advantage.
- Declining margins, escalating costs.

There are only two things that money cannot buy these days – Time and Friends.
Comment by GM Executive in his late-40s, explaining why he chose early retirement.

Facing challenges such as these, how would you have reacted to someone suggesting you restructure the organization? Probably with: "Not now – can't you see I'm busy!!??"

Yet if you were able to stop treading water long enough, responding to these changes in your business environments will likely deliver the biggest long-term pay-off in most cases. So why can't you successfully instigate change?

In my experience, most corporations are unable to successfully deal with change because of two over-riding reasons:

1. They lack the cohesive strength of a corporate soul, a spirit based on shared values and goals;

2. They are hamstrung by an obsolete organizational structure which not only prevents easy change but actually discourages it by its very architecture.

I've touched on this aspect of a corporate soul and plan to return to it later. Right now, let's deal with that favorite subject of management consultants everywhere, the corporate structure.

Like their original models – the military organization and the Catholic church – the classic organizational structure of business organizations was a pyramid. From its wide, solid and immovable base, the corporate pyramid tapered at a fixed angle upwards toward a single individual who was ultimately responsible for the success of the organization. Hey, it worked in Egypt for 5000 years, right?

Two or three decades ago business leaders realized that, while pyramids are fine structures for stability, they weren't much on flexibility and they weren't the best model to use when responding to a buyer's market. That's because customers dealt only with employees forming the bottom row of stones; the base of the pyramid expanded to meet an increase in the number of customers whose patronage made the pyramid possible. In fact, the wider the base, the higher the tip of the pyramid and the more remote from the ground was its occupant.

Far-sighted business consultants examined the pyramid structure more closely and identified a number of serious problems with the original pyramid structure. For one thing, it was irresponsible because all the direction came from the top and all the action – at least as far as changing tastes and customer expectations were concerned – took place down among the sand dunes.

The pyramid's very structure says "This is a hierarchy, and don't you forget it!" Critical news, like a change in buyer tastes and subtle yet important shifts in attitude, moved up from the bottom, growing more and more exhausted until it reached the peak.

As a splendid palace deserted by its inhabitants looks like a ruin, so does a man without character, all his material belongings notwithstanding.

Gandhi

Meanwhile, executive decisions moved down from the top, growing less and less effective with every level until they reached the real world at the grass-roots level. By the time top management became aware that customer needs were not being satisfied, the customers had wandered further into the desert.

Gernon's First Law of Communication. Every time information changes hands it also changes shape.

Gernon's Second Law of Communication. Expect to be misunderstood and you'll seldom be disappointed.

And even when an honest-to-goodness mover-and-shaker found himself at the peak of the pyramid, he discovered that his biggest enemy was inertia. Well, what did they expect? Pyramids have sat immobile in the Sahara for 30 or 40 centuries. Don't try to move one to downtown Cairo, let alone Wall Street or Peoria. They're there to stay.

Rome fell because of a leaching away of meaning, and loss of faith.
Lewis Mumford

But I was never entirely satisfied with the image. And neither, I realized, were many of the client staff who attended my management training sessions.

So business gurus began suggesting that pyramid structures must be turned literally upside down. Soon the phrase "Inverted Pyramid" became as commonplace as "The Paperless Office" ... and its benefits just as elusive.

The inverted pyramid – in theory at least – places all those individuals and job functions who maintain direct contact with customers at the top of the pyramid. The base of the pyramid with, it is assumed, the entire weight of the organization pressing upon him or her, would now be represented by the CEO.

This concept grew very popular in the late 1980s, a spin-off from the new doctrine of Customer Focus. I must admit that I subscribed to it as well; it seemed an effective method of demonstrating the need to restructure an organization, and draw attention to the needs of customers over those of management. For one thing, an inverted pyramid looks terribly unstable. Talk all you want about dynamics and flexibility, neither is effective in a corporate setting unless everyone feels confident that the organization will survive the next stiff breeze . . . and an inverted pyramid clearly will not.

(I know, I know, it's only a visual concept, the graphic representation of a philosophical idea. But hasn't a niggling little voice at the back of your mind asked, whenever faced with the infamous inverted pyramid image: "What the heck's holding it up?")

Also, the inverted pyramid had little effect on middle managers who, in my experience, were usually the biggest obstacle to meaningful corporate change. Upright or inverted, middle managers remained in the same relative position within the pyramid; smack in the center, distanced from customers and ultimately responsive only to those nearest the tip.

Proving once again that youth is wasted on the young . . . According to the UCLA Graduate School of Education, 97% of U.S. kindergarten children think creatively; only 3% form thoughts in a conforming, structured manner. By the end of high school, only 46% think creatively; the rest prefer a rigid, structured style. And at age 30, only 3% of Americans enjoy the freedom to think for themselves – the rest screen their thinking according to orthodoxy and social correctness.

Companies pointed to their new organizational structure with pride but the flow was still one way: from the tip of the pyramid towards the base. The same levels of the company remained in close contact with the customer; and the same executive decisions were made at a distance from those customers.

Let me point out that the failure of the inverted pyramid structure was rarely, if ever, due to lack of a sincere intent to change on the part of virtually everyone. I have sat in meetings with CEOs who almost implored me to submit a never-fail formula for change. "This company needs a shake-up," they would say. "We have to get better, we have to get flexible, become more responsive." In meetings with employee groups, I would hear the same lyrics sung in a slightly different key. "We can do better," the staff might say.

"We've got a good product and good people, but we're not doing the best work we're capable of. Help us change!"

This was good news, and usually meant that my proposals would be taken seriously and implemented quickly. In fact, they usually were.

But there were nagging times when something else happened – when, as sincere as the intent might be, *the will to change simply wasn't present*. This was disturbing. How could an entire company want to change, be committed to change – but be unable to succeed?

The answer lay in two aspects of these companies.

One was a stubborn insistence – usually, I'm afraid to say, by middle managers – on clinging to one of the few things these people assumed were permanent and immutable: the organizational structure.

Now, I understand basic psychology. I could see why they were acting this way. The people in these companies were being battered, and in the midst of a storm, you cling to the nearest solid thing at hand. So we had middle managers faced with change from every direction – technological change, social change, economic change, even change in the way they had plotted their careers (Can you say "plateaued"?) – and the only thing that gave them comfort was their position within the organization. If they could freeze their position, their duties and their responsibilities, they could establish a solid location for riding out the storm until at least retirement.

But while every middle manager had a reason to feel that way, not all of them did.

The ones who embraced change, to the degree that they felt confident enough to commit their careers to it, were employed by companies who boasted a shared spirit, a visionary sense of purpose . . . a corporate soul.

Permit me to inject another note of theology here.

Our works do not ennoble us; but we must ennoble our works.

Meister Eckhart

He who stands for nothing will fall for anything.

We have all known friends, family, acquaintances and business associates who faced serious personal crises. From the sudden loss of a job or a spouse to the tragic death of a child, these crises often seemed too large, too unfair and too incomprehensible for any one individual to bear. Some did, with inspiring strength, rising above the crisis to resume their lives. Others didn't; they slipped into a cycle of depression and paralysis, and tragedy began to pile upon tragedy.

What made the difference?

In my opinion, it depends on whether the individual who suffered the loss followed a set of core values and beliefs strong enough to remain unshaken by the shattering event. The core was their grounding point, their anchor, their compass, whatever you wish to call it. In one way or another, this "core" concept reflects spiritual values in the widest sense of the term. Whether based on an organized faith or deeply rooted in a personal moralistic creed, it works the same way and provides the same essential benefits.

Corporations are not all that different from people. They both have distinct personalities, special talents, definable life cycles and other common traits. If that's the case, they can also have a soul. Which means they adhere to a core system of values and beliefs.

These corporations are clearly advantaged when faced with a crisis of any size. Their response in stressful situations – such as change on a grand scale – tends to reflect those of a deeply spiritual person or a member of an organized religion:

- They tighten their grip on a tradition and sense of values.
- They gather closely together, supporting each other.
- They take the long view: "This too shall pass."
- They review their core beliefs.
- They work harder than ever to move past the challenge and towards abundance again.

The deepest principle of human nature is the craving to be appreciated.
William James

Think of the companies that have regrouped in the face of major challenges of many kinds. The obvious ones include:

Caterpillar	Chrysler	Disney
Harley-Davidson	Hewlett-Packard	IBM
John Deere	Xerox	

When you think of these corporations, you usually picture a company whose core values and sense of duty (now there's an old-fashioned word, but I think it's appropriate in this context) are clearly defined.

We are put on this earth not to see through one another, but to see one another through.
Peter De Vries

Some, such as Disney and Harley-Davidson, have had to reassess themselves, reflect on what they stand for, and rededicate themselves to their core function. Others, like Chrysler and IBM, re-invented themselves to one extent or another; they didn't change their principal products, but they certainly changed the way the products were delivered.

A few gathered by the river, reaffirmed their faith, re-read their bibles and rolled up their sleeves – here I think of Caterpillar (who survived a very long and bitter strike, determined to build on its export potential) ; Xerox (who, as we saw, were able to shift gears and get the bus moving again without having all the passengers disembark first); and John Deere (who drew upon decades of loyalty among its dealer and customer base, using it to ride out a market that destroyed much of its competition).

Clearly, the first step in restructuring is to *strengthen the spirit* – determine who and what you are, and draw upon your "soulful center."

Above all, admit to yourself that <u>no meaningful change can be achieved without a sense of security among every member of your organization</u>. Or, to put it another way:

How can your team keep their eye on the ball if they're always looking over their shoulder?

If pyramids place the decision-making process too far from the customer, and if inverted pyramids generate instability and continued isolation for middle managers, what is the new paradigm for the 21st century?

I suggest a doughnut, or perhaps a bagel.

Hear me out:

Be confident in making your needs known to one another, for each of you, to the extent that God grants you grace, should nourish and love one another as a mother loves and nourishes her child.

St. Francis of Assisi

The problem with the inverted pyramid structure wasn't intent; customer focus was, and still is, the key to success in today's rapidly changing market. Henry Ford's dictum about his Model T – "You can have any color you want as long as it's black" – is as outdated and unsound (when judged by today's standards) as the cars that rolled off his assembly lines. If consumers decide they want ochre-colored Oldsmobiles next year, you can bet that Oldsmobiles will roll off the line in awesome shades of ochre. That's the power of response to customer preference.

The inverted pyramid, as we have seen, failed in part because it still isolated key decision-making levels from the customers and because it was inherently unstable.

So do this:

Draw a small circle in the middle of the page:

Your customer

This is where your customer resides. This your customer's world. Forget the board room, the shop steward, the shipping dock and the country club. Your customers are here. Your customers make their buying decisions in their space, and if you're not nearby, you're not in the picture.

A business that makes nothing but money is a poor kind of business.
Henry Ford

Now draw a larger circle around the first one.

The space between the circles is where your corporate functions occur – as many as possible in direct proximity to the customer. Within that space, draw a series of small pyramids – the upright kind with a solid, stable foundation. Each pyramid represents a function or department within your company – sales, production, service, whatever – structured to keep the decision-maker for that function near the customer.

Notice also that the doughnut diagram positions the customer at the center of all your firm's actions and activities. It also suggests an interesting definition of achievement that the pyramid concept avoids:

He who serves most is most successful. And, incidentally, is positioned best to receive direct feedback.

It takes more than a revised diagram to position a company for a change to true customer-focused operation. That's where the ten-step process comes in, as detailed in Chapter 14.

But first, let's suggest some activities and deal with questions of quality and continuous improvement.

Great men are they who see that spiritual power is stronger than material force – that thoughts rule the world.

Ralph Waldo Emerson

ACTIVITIES

1. All companies have qualities that provide both stability and instability. Identify yours, and decide if they represent a mild, medium or serious problem to your staff morale.

1._____☐*Mild* ☐*Medium* ☐*Serious*
2._____☐*Mild* ☐*Medium* ☐*Serious*
3._____☐*Mild* ☐*Medium* ☐*Serious*
4._____☐*Mild* ☐*Medium* ☐*Serious*
5._____☐*Mild* ☐*Medium* ☐*Serious*

2. I listed some prominent firms which either drew upon or recreated their shared spirit or corporate soul. Do you know of any local firms which have achieved the same thing? Write three here:

1. _____

2. _____

3. _____

3. Draw the "doughnut" – make it reasonably large (at least three inches in diameter) and add as many pyramids as your company would need within the doughnut – each pyramid representing a service, function or department directly related to customer needs and activities.

CHAPTER 13

Big Ideas

Big Idea #1: Creating a corporate soul requires shifting to a new set of values and time horizons.

A too short-term focus produces "Corporate Anorexia."

Big Idea #2: Believing in a corporate soul often requires a leap of faith.

What can we hold on to as we leap? Where can we find security during the uncomfortable elements of the change process?

CHAPTER 13

Before You Climb a Mountain, You Have to Trust the Rope.

The character of an organization is often embodied in the CEO. Kelvin Browne has identified the following negative qualities of a CEO:

PROFILE – *Beware of a boss who maintains a high profile by appearing regularly on the covers of business magazines and is frequently quoted in newspapers. "The boss's insatiable quest for notoriety means that everything you do must reflect favorably on the CEO," warns Browne.*

AGE – *Companies headed by people under 40 or over 60 are not good places to be employed according to Browne. "(Those)" under 40 are probably very ambitious and compensate for lack of experience with ruthlessness."*

CEOs over age 60 are also a problem; Browne suggests they're too busy thinking about their retirement to worry about the mid-term future of the company.

(cont. on the next page)

The concept of a corporation possessing a soul or spirit is the most natural thing in the world. The only *unnatural* aspect is the way some people tend to ignore or ridicule the idea when it's in their interests.

Corporations are based on their recognition as a separate legal entity. This is very handy when it comes to financial concerns such as taxation, stock ownership, profits and dividends. That's when every CEO agrees with the Oxford Dictionary's legal definition of a corporation as "an artificial person created by royal charter, prescription or legislative act and having the capacity of perpetual succession." (In case there's any other confusion of a corporation's entity, let's remember the Latin root *corporal*: "of or belonging to a body").

So a corporation is an entity, a body, an identity in at least a legal sense. But can it have a personality? You know it can. And so do the CEOs of corporations ranging from Apple to Zenith who spend millions each year in advertising to identify their firms not by the products they offer but by the way they do business – their ethics, their reputation, their responsiveness, their plans for the future and their attempts at filling the role of good citizens.

SHAREHOLDINGS – *Think a CEO with large chunks of public stock in the company is a good bet? Think again.*

"They may bleed a company if they need to pay dividends and they will slash jobs, including yours, for short-term gain."

Browne concludes:

"The unspoken quality of an ideal CEO is one who makes his or her decisions on the basis of a widely-held set of values designed to lead the organization toward a long-term goal which will benefit all of its supporters and participants."

Add them up and that's a personality.

The key question is: what kind of soul exists within the personality of your organization – Mother Teresa or Charles Manson?

The idea isn't frivolous. Nor is it meant to be intentionally provocative.

The actions and values of Mother Teresa aren't focused on the end of the week or next month; her actions are measured in much longer periods. Charles Manson, like virtually every convicted criminal, sane or insane, has a much shorter time span in mind. (Talk to any criminologist and they'll agree that the most common element among criminals isn't their intelligence, social standing or even their moral values; it's their inability to recognize the consequences of their actions, because they cannot see beyond immediate gratification.)

Saints, as writer James Salter reminds us, keep their eye on things eternal in nature. Sinners are more concerned about temporal matters and let's admit it . . . we're all sinners.

In other words, one of the distinctions between the extremes of souls is the contrast in perception of *time.*

Yet this is the area in which most North American corporations are woefully short-sighted. *Until companies extend their time-frames far enough ahead for employees to feel reasonably comfortable and secure in their positions, no meaningful change can or will occur.*

Science without religion is lame, and religion without science is blind.

Albert Einstein

I think that maybe in every company today, there is at least one person who is slowly going crazy.

Joseph Heller

Time frames for both corporations and individuals have been shrinking over the past two decades until both are now dominated by the quarterly financial statement.

The quarterly financial period became the norm when banks and other financial groups began demanding that corporations account for their performance every 90 days. As a result, everything lives or dies according to the financial quarter period. A slipping performance in one quarter means the bank will have their accounting microscopes well-polished for the next quarter. Lose money for two quarters in a row and the corporation feels the heat; show a loss for three quarters in a row and the CEO feels the heat, leading to the dreaded "I screwed up and you have to pay" syndrome among company bosses.

At best, this leads to a lessening ability to focus on opportunities which may lie on the far horizon. At worst, it produces debacles like the bankruptcy of Orange County, California. You may recall that the treasurer of Orange County manipulated a $7.5 billion portfolio to include such unusual investments as inverse floating derivatives to meet the county's quarterly performance goals. The result was a loss of over one-and-a-half billion dollars from the county's assets and the disappearance of 700 county jobs. (Among the losses were 129 jobs, 98 telephones, 6 fax machines and 10 cellular telephones from the sheriff's department. This produced a leap in crime statistics in Orange County, which yielded an even more difficult hurdle for administrators when it came to bailing the county out of its morass. Does the term "vicious cycle" mean anything to you?)

I'm not suggesting that companies discard regular assessments of their financial performance. Among other reasons, Chase Manhattan would probably disagree with me and that's one disagreement I couldn't expect to win. I am suggesting, however, that corporations must begin wearing bifocals for both short and long-term assessment of their progress *because whether it's saving the environment or saving your own soul, the 90-day formula just doesn't work.*

You can't measure environmental progress in 90-day increments. It took 100 years to mess up Canada's Great Lakes; it will take more than 100 days to clean them up.

And you will not enrich the lives of your employees by focusing on downsizing, de-layering, restructuring or any other euphemism you can name. Short-term perspectives do not benefit society, they demean it by any measure you may choose.

One business consultant I know describes the perpetual down-sizing of business as "Corporate Anorexia." It produces a slim, hard individual with no reserves of nutrition or strength, one that is whirling out of balance internally. In business, we call down-sizing

When a man says he got rich through hard work, ask him "Whose?"
Don Marquis

An atheist is a man with no visible means of support.
Lord Tweedsmuir

a trend or a strategy; in medicine, it's a serious disease.

For several hundred years, philosophers and social scientists have agreed that a healthy individual manages to balance aspects of both the personality and the soul. It is the soul which reflects on one's place in society and concern for fellow human beings; it is the personality which fantasizes about a new car, a new watch, a new spouse. The soul sees its place in eternity; the personality sees its dreams filled on payday. The soul deals in self-worth; the personality measures its gains in net worth.

Thus we are out of balance, as individuals and corporations, if our achievements are related to our personalities exclusively.

Earlier, I mentioned the dramatic difference between companies that sincerely wanted change and took steps to implement it. Some succeeded easily while others fell far short of their expectations.

Invariably, the difference could be measured according to the degree of security and confidence felt by the employees. The image that comes to mind when comparing the two groups is one of a novice rock climber or mountaineer. I picture someone attempting to scale a great height and already several hundred feet off the ground. Above them (you can tell I'm following a traditional pyramid structure here), their mountaineering guide is instructing them what to do. The guide knows the way, he has scaled the same rock face, he is in a position to see more (albeit in a safer location) and the only way you can join him is by following his instruction.

So picture yourself hanging by a rope.

In one instance, you have been told that the rope is strong enough and securely tied to support ten times your weight. No matter how much force you can place on that rope, you simply cannot break it. The guide above you says: "The way up is by swinging out from the face of the mountain, dangling in mid-air by the rope and coming back in further down the face." If the rope holds, what have you lost? And the rope *will* hold; you have no doubt about that.

Imagine yourself on the same mountain face, with a different climbing guide and equipment outfitter. All you know about the rope that is preventing you from tumbling into the valley is that it was purchased from the lowest bidder. And all the guide tells you from above is something like: "Kick-out, hold on and change your position if you want any hope of surviving."

Now I don't know about you, but I'd stay where I was as long as I could. If told to change my position, I'm not going to kick out very far because it might put too much strain on this rope I'm clinging to. In fact, I'm not sure I want to change anything at all. Lower my food down in a bucket; I just might remain where I am as long as I can. In one piece.

That's the mind-set I often see in employees of corporations who claim to be gearing up for change. They don't want to move. They're afraid to kick out. *They don't trust the rope.*

The Ten Steps to Change in the following chapters will prove as effective as your employees feel secure.

True security is not measured by the number of locks on your door or the size of the gun under your pillow. It is measured by the status of your belief in yourself and in the values which guide your behavior.

Who feels more secure when they close their eyes at night: Mother Teresa or Charles Manson?

That's the power of spiritual values. And why they are a key element in fostering meaningful change in any organization.

Change is a natural progression of development and is not a threat to the secure believer. An absence of secure belief in the long-term values of an organization is an insurmountable barrier to change.

ACTIVITIES
1. What corporate character traits are revealed in your CEO?

2. What aspects of your organization's corporate culture reinforce short term thinking and temporal values?

3. What aspects of your organization's corporate culture reinforce long term vision and values?

CHAPTER 14

Big Ideas

Big Idea #1: The hierarchical approach to planning and implementing change has given way to a superior technology . . . the team process.

Big Idea #2: To be effective change must be built on the following foundation principles:
1. The climate/culture must support the change.
2. Teams must be used to plan and manage every aspect of the change process.
But team members must function according to the Four Commandments if they hope to be effective.

CHAPTER 14

Preparing for Change: Can You Really Grow Cotton in Saskatchewan?

Our Mission
To boldly go where no one has gone before.

So many things have changed that even the way we prepare for change has changed!

It's true. A decade or so ago, corporations launched new programs, systems, divisions – anything to do with change – using the same techniques employed by Alexander the great when plotting a battle. Senior management would get together and review the steps to be taken. Then, middle managers would attend seminars to be indoctrinated in the changes approved by senior managers. The middle managers would return to their departments with stars in their eyes and fire in their bellies to pass the gospel on to supervisors, who functioned as a conduit to the rest of the staff.

Their's not to question why.
Their's but to do and die.
Into the valley of death.
Rode the six hundred.
Alfred, Lord Tennyson,
The Charge of the Light Brigade

It was all very linear, following a chain of command from top to bottom. Unfortunately, the results were often reminiscent of the parlor game in which one person sitting in a circle whispers "Johnny has a bag of jelly beans" into someone's ear, who passes on the message to the next person in the circle and so on. By the time the original message returns to its starting point, Johnny and the jelly beans have been transformed into nasty things some people do to camels, or some other outrageous thought.

Even with all the corporate communications tools in place and humming – video presentations, newsletters, banners, posters and buttons – by the time the new gospel according to management reaches the shop floor or the sales floor, it bears little resemblance to the original premise. What began as starry eyes and fiery bellies becomes nothing more than myopia and heart burn.

The weaker the corporate soul, the more likely this old pattern of change management will not only fail, but backfire. Instead of change, the result is more likely to be escalating cynicism and heightened resistance. Many reasons exist for this phenomenon, and I suspect that none of them will come as a total surprise to you.

Gernon's Rules of Corporate Communication:

1. *Every time information changes hands, it also changes shape.*
2. *Expect to be misunderstood and you'll seldom be disappointed.*

One factor is distance. Remember "The person nearest the problem is best equipped to solve it"? Every employee knows this instinctively; many managers forget it as they rise through the ranks. The corollary of this might be expressed as: "Wisdom is reduced by a factor of two for every level it is removed from its target." (I think there is a similar physics formula to this, but I'm not sure.) In any case, linear directives regarding change are the weakest possible method of communication in any organization, especially one lacking in a unifying system of beliefs and values.

But the stronger the shared corporate spirit, the greater the impact of effective change at every level.

"Come to the edge," he said. They said, "But we are afraid." "Come to the edge," he said. They came. And he pushed them. And they flew.
Guillaume Apollinaire

How is having a smoking section in a restaurant different from having a peeing section in a swimming pool?

With a strong, shared corporate spirit, change can be implemented not by linear directive or legislation, but by instinct and osmosis.

Happily, several models exist to prove this theory, within both successful progressive companies and society at large. Consider smoking and drinking, for example. Only a generation or two ago, both were not only socially acceptable activities; they also indicated levels of sophistication and social standing. Watch a late-show movie from the 50s and 60s, or just try to picture Humphrey Bogart in a white dinner jacket without a cigarette in his hand and a glass of whiskey nearby.

Controls existed on tobacco and alcohol. But any government body which attempted to prevent people from smoking at their workplace would have been condemned as draconian in its view and trounced at the next elections.

Until the 1990s, of course.

By then, North American society had acquired a new system of values, a shared spirit that rejected the idea of tobacco as anything more than an unhealthy habit destructive not only to the smoker but to those in the immediate vicinity. Today, some government bodies are proposing that adults who choose to smoke in their own homes with youngsters present could be guilty of child abuse – and no one is outraged at the concept.

Our attitude towards alcohol has changed as well. At one time, drunk drivers were the butt of jokes, like someone who has committed a social faux pas. But too many tragic deaths and too much slaughter on the highways generated a new shared spirit. The change, sometimes dictated by government bodies, sometimes inspired by citizens groups, produced Designated Drivers, jail terms for driving while intoxicated, and a generally low tolerance for anyone who climbs behind the wheel of a vehicle with alcohol in his or her blood.

None of these changes could have occurred unless a shared spirit, a washing wave of social awareness, had swept over the majority of ordinary people, creating a positive atmosphere for revisions to be made. If profits are the harvest your organization reaps from all its activities, before you change your crop to a richer bounty, you better make certain you have the climate to support it. Or to put it another way: Don't expect to grow cotton in Saskatchewan.

Permit me to return to Japan for a moment.

Among the key differences between North American and Japanese management techniques is the number of employees each manager supervises. In North America, it's now about 15; in Japan, it's around 150. That means the span of control between their management technique and our own is extended 10 times.

It is no use walking anywhere to preach unless the walking is the preaching.

St. Francis of Assisi

Conventional retailers trained for a sale; we train for knowledge. They train with an eye on the balance sheet; we train with an eye on the soul.

*Anita Roddick
Co-Founder,
The Body Shop*

Are Japanese managers that much more effective in communicating goals and processes? Not really. It simply proves that Japanese corporations are far more successful at generating and nurturing shared values at multiple levels, leaving individual employees to manage themselves. Directives are not imposed; they are created and communicated within the limits of shared values.

Don't just empower individuals; empower teams.

The more complex our life and work become, the higher the value we should place on teamwork. Nine times out of ten, teams make wiser decisions and function more effectively than individuals; the lone genius may make a breakthrough in perception and creativity, but it almost always takes a team to turn a brainstorm into a deluge of ideas.

Unfortunately, while many executives are able to accept the effectiveness of empowerment for individuals, many have a severe problem in awarding the same authority to teams. Providing this kind of opportunity for teams in a time of change may take an act of faith, but it is clearly essential. Few endeavors in life are more assured of success than those tackled by a dedicated team whose members all share the same values. Under these conditions, Buckminster Fuller's definition of synergy – "When 2+2=5" – evolves from a provocative statement to practical proof.

Earlier, I stated that teams outperform individuals in making critical decisions at least nine times out of ten. That's not merely a guesstimate on my part, it's an accurate assessment based on experience with team-building exercises. One of the most popular of these exercises consists of a survival game. The premises of the game consists of challenging survivors of an airplane crash in the desert or the Arctic to rate, in order of value, fifteen items they were able to salvage before the aircraft wreckage exploded in flame. The actual list varies, but typically may consist of:

- Compass
- Cigarette lighter that is out of fuel
- Two foot-long inch-thick wooden boards.
- Paper stapler
- Letter opener
- Newspaper
  . . . and so on.

Participants are directed to rate the value of these items in descending order as individuals. Then, forming teams, they are asked to rate the items again. Survival experts have already ranked the items in order of true value where it counts – in the middle of the Sahara or in the midst of an Arctic blizzard, depending on the scenario – and the individual and team responses are compared with the expert view.

Here's where teams achieve the 90% improvement record over individuals. As individuals, each participant carries within him or her a unique mix of knowledge and ignorance. But as a team this matrix overlaps, and one person's experience fills the gap existing from another person's unawareness.

For example, in an Arctic crash simulation, most people opt for a compass immediately. But within the Arctic Circle, compasses can be seriously inaccurate in determining true north, due to the difference between the North Pole and the magnetic north, so the instrument's value is immediately diminished. Similarly, the lighter without fluid can still be valuable if it generates a spark to light flares or other contrivances.

Here's another take on the "nine out of ten" score for teams:

The statistic also proves that once out of ten times, an individual scores better than the team. So why not begin by looking for that person? Well, that generates a problem of its own. Usually, either everybody on the team thinks "I'm that person – I can find the solution!" or they think "I'm not that person – don't expect me to be a hero!" Of course, in the survival game if someone says "I'm the person" and he or she is not . . . everybody dies.

Personally, I'd rather rely on team decisions.

The best of teams in this exercise, and in virtually all the real-life situations upon which it is based, actually do yield more skills than expected from the group when the members are assessed as individuals. It's as though an

Love alone is capable of uniting living beings in such a way as to complete and fulfill them, for it alone takes them and joins them by what is deepest in themselves. Does not love every instant achieve all around us in the couple or the team, the magic feat of personalizing by totalizing?

Pierre Teilhard de Chardin

invisible person has been added to the team, someone whose presence is not apparent until the team begins scoring successes, or when the members reflect on the process later.

All right, I'll say it: What happens is the birth of a spirit, a soul comprised of shared identity, which manages to strengthen the individuals in their decision-making and add resolve to the team in their actions. It's real, it exists, and it is the hidden force behind the success of team empowerment.

The Varying Value of Successful Teams.

Teams are the key to managing and implementing successful change within an organization, but they are not the sole solution. The value of a team varies according to the nature of the problem being dealt with. Here are four observations regarding team function with regard to change management:

1. *Teams are most valuable when the path is unplotted and the methodology is unclear.* Think of the first few moments following a disaster, such as an air crash, when the survivors gather and assess their situation.

2. *As the path becomes clearer and a quality plan emerges, the team's role will be gradually reduced or may shift its emphasis.* You and your companions are trekking along a trail towards food and shelter, leaving the disaster site behind; the team is still important in many ways, but it is no longer as critical to your survival.

3. *A mediocre team solution is usually more effective than a "perfect" solution imposed from elsewhere.* Consider a football team on the field during a critical point in an important game. The quarterback – the team leader – has heard comments from other players about the situation. One member of the other team seems to be hurting, another is almost impregnable, the field on the far side is unusually slippery, and so on. Based on this, the quarterback calls a play designed to move the ball ten yards. Then, from the sideline, a player brings a play from the coach that's expected to score a touchdown. Which one do you think the team will believe in most? Which one is likely to be successful?

4. *Learning to work as an effective team takes time and training. Management's role is to ensure that quality decisions are made.* That's basic. But all of the decisions to be made in a teamwork environment must recognize the dynamics of an effective team process. Not all solutions made by a new team will be of the highest quality at the beginning. This doesn't suggest that the team is either ineffective or incompetent; it simply indicates that teamwork, like any other skill, takes practice to develop.

Adopt the pace of nature. Her secret is patience.

Ralph Waldo Emerson

Gernon's Four Commandments Of Applying Teamwork To Change.

It should be obvious to you that I'm not in favor of a dictatorial approach to any management activity, but I urge you to follow these four guidelines for teams involved in change management:

1. **Agree on the process needed to deal with the problem at hand.** This represents a basic stumbling block for many teams, even though its importance may be readily apparent. Upon first meeting, a team may have as many problem-solving processes available as there are team members. If each member follows his or her pet process, the entire team will be out of step with each other.

   Going back to the survival game I mentioned earlier, consider the alternatives available to the team members: Stick together or separate? Stay put or walk out? Escape or survive? These are process decisions, and unless the team agrees on one or the other, their success is seriously threatened.

2. **Team members must actively listen to one another.** The only way to secure full participation in the process is by encouraging every member to contribute his or her views – especially at the outset. Some views will be unpopular or impractical, but they must be heard and evaluated.

Searching for quality ideas is like prospecting for gold. You may have to turn over a lot of rock to get to the gold.

Whoever makes the fewest persons uneasy is the best bred in the company.
Jonathan Swift

Trust the Force, Luke
Obiwan to Luke in
<u>Star Wars</u>

Trust the System.
Bob Gernon to you in
real life

3. **Team members must learn how to confront and disagree with each other, while avoiding any personal attacks.**

4. **Team members must learn to support and build one another up.** This is the other side of point. Confrontation and disagreement will not be destructive if every member truly believes that the other members support him or her, drawing on the unique abilities of each member and helping to build self-esteem.

A number of dynamics are at work here, and I understand it if you detect the aroma of potential anarchy in all of this. That's not the case, if the process is seen to be one that is equal parts of practical action and spiritual belief.

Part of the belief process is to acknowledge the true value of every other person on the team. When you value others around you – seeing them as critical contributors to your personal success and the overall success of the team – it becomes much easier to talk to them reasonably and listen to them attentively.

Spirit holds the team together, and guides them in the process. The stronger the shared spirit, the more effective the team will be in managing themselves and achieving their goals.

A Cautionary Tale about Assumptions and Directives.

Earlier, I mentioned the importance of empowering teams and the dangers of assuming tight control over their decision-making process. A superb example of this arose several years ago during a training session with a major international corporation.

I was using the survival game, setting out the situation – a crash-landing in the desert with limited gear available to the team.

The teams were challenged to make decisions *as a team* leading to their success.

One team included a senior manager who immediately assumed control. He was a World War Two veteran, having served in desert combat. "I've been there," he told the other members. "I know what to do." All the other team members, respectful of his position and experience, immediately gave in. There was no team structure and no teamwork. The executive made all the decisions and sat back confidently while his score was determined.

The score was dreadful, lowest by far of all the other teams. The executive was embarrassed, and the reasons for his failure were obvious.

He had made his decisions based on two critical assumptions, neither of which would have been shared by other team members. 1) He assumed that it was war time – which is when he obtained his training and experience.

Under battle conditions, you may very well crash behind enemy lines, so to avoid capture you keep moving. But no one has said this was a war-time situation. The executive was frozen in his own assumptions. His decision to abandon the crash site was wrong – fatally wrong in the opinion of survival experts. 2) He also assumed that he was in his early 20s – his age when he served in the army. But that was then, and this was now. "Now" meant he was more than 40 years older, and the prospect of a man in his mid-60s crossing the desert without guidance or extensive survival gear would be disastrous.

Had the army veteran listened attentively to the views of others, weighing them against reality and not unspoken assumptions, he would surely have altered his decisions. Fortunately, this wasn't real life. Instead of sacrificing the lives of every member of the team, he was merely humiliated.

ACTIVITIES

1. What, in your opinion, are two or three major weaknesses of top-down driven change?

2. What is the "span of control" of managers within your organization? i.e., How many "direct reports" is the average? Does this need to be changed?

3. What guiding principles/commandments could be followed by planning or problem solving teams?

CHAPTER 15

Big Ideas

Big Idea #1: Learn what the two key functions of an effective transformation process are.

Big Idea #2: Learn why the traditional approach to organizational change does not work when it comes to building a circular organization.

Big Idea #3: Learn why a leap-of-faith is essential to starting the transformation process.

CHAPTER 15

Letting Go . . .
The First Step in Transformation.

Life is largely a matter of expectation.
Horace

The transformation process consists of two distinct functions: The first is Steering. The second is Design.

1. Steering refers to the process of setting and communicating the overall direction and ensuring that everyone (all resources invested) moves the organization persistently in that direction.

2. Design relates to the process of creating and implementing specific actions to capitalize on the priority problems/opportunities in the Steering process.

Two Teams for Two Different Functions

We tend to get what we expect.
N. V. Peal

Note that it takes two different teams to effectively manage the transformation. In the past, corporate transformations were launched in a traditional and usually ineffective manner, that went something like this:

1. Owners or top management agree that a "Team-based, customer-centered, total-quality organization" is the goal. So . . .

2. Various selected managers are sent off to a seminar lasting two days or two weeks or somewhere in between. Then . . .

The person Interested in success has to learn to view failure as a healthy inevitable part of the process of getting to the top.
Dr. Joyce Brothers

Failure is only the opportunity to more intelligently begin again.
Henry Ford

3. Assuming the seminar is successful, and the managers are convinced that quality improvement and wide participation is the route to follow, they return brimming with knowledge and enthusiasm, with the goal of . . .

4. Converting their old rigid, hierarchical organizations into flexible, team-based, customer-centered, circular ones.

5. Each manager pulls everyone in his or her department together for a motivational meeting in which they passionately outline the New Vision and direction.

6. The employees grow enthusiastic, perhaps hopeful and certainly relieved. Publicly, they express their commitment to the program. Privately, they wonder why it took so long for "the people upstairs" to reach a conclusion that virtually everyone else had reached years earlier. But back to the managers.

The above process sounds reasonable so far, so why is it doomed to failure? Read on.

Our newly trained managers return from their seminar almost certainly facing a heavier workload than they left behind, for now they are confronted with the day-to-day tasks of management plus a backlog of decisions, reports, assessments and reviews that has accumulated in their absence. At the same time, they have the added assignment of launching the turn-

When motivated to go in two directions at the same time . . . you go nowhere.

It is impossible to ride two horses to the finish line.
René Louvat

He that does good to another does good also to himself.
Seneca

around that will save their organizations and lead to greater levels of achievement and success in the future.

So the managers in question, fueled by enthusiasm from the new direction and genuine commitment to the betterment of the organization, determine to devote say . . . 10 or 20 percent of their time to this critical changeover program.

But wait a minute. It took at least 100 percent of the managers' daily time to handle the daily tasks in the old hierarchical structure. How can they convert from a pyramid to a circle with just 20 percent of their time? Especially when you consider that converting to the circle format is a mid-to-long term goal (i.e., low priority); while operating the existing hierarchy is a short-term and high priority project. Good intentions or not, it's easy to understand how maintaining the existing structure takes precedence over converting it to the desired version. For it is the existing structure that generates the daily outputs essential to short-, mid- and long-term success.

The challenge they face is akin to driving a bus and changing all the tires at the same time . . . without stopping. Pretty soon the enthusiasm born from the seminar begins to wane. There just isn't enough time and energy to do everything. Fears grow that, without constant attention, the existing pyramid structure may collapse before it is converted to a circular format. So in the heat of the battle, managers shift their attention to short-term survival issues. They promise to return to the goals of the transformation process just as soon as this latest brush fire is extinguished . . . right after the quarterly report is completed . . . immediately following the break-in period for the new computer program . . . and so on.

The employees? They feel demoralized, abandoned and deceived. Empty promises are worse than none at all. Their managers lose credibility in their eyes. Cynicism runs rampant and skepticism grows to enormous proportions.

He who wished to secure the good of others, has already secured his own.
Confucius

Welcome to the Catch-22 of managing corporate change. It goes like this:
- The Leader is <u>responsible</u> for change, <u>yet</u>

Help thy brother's boat across, and lo! Thine own has reached the shore.
Hindu Proverb

- The Leader cannot make the change happen him/herself, but . . .
- The Leader <u>can halt change</u> by not supporting it consistently.

Doesn't that sound like an impossible task? The classic double-bind of being responsible for something over which you have no control? So where's the hope? What can be done?

Fortunately, here's where team dynamics, total participation and all of the values and beliefs covered in the previous chapters enter the picture.

Step 1: A Leap of Faith

I believe that you can get everything you want if you will help enough other people get what they want.
Zig Ziglar

The first step in the transformation process is a <u>leap of faith</u> that entails the manager admitting he/she is helpless to make the change happen. The first requirement is for the manager to <u>give</u>

Faith is based upon some-thing – the evidence of things not seen. To have faith, we must have evi-dence. Faith is not blind. We can know the invisible by seeing the visible. We can see the trees bend and know there is wind. We can see the moon re-flect light and name it "shining."
Wynn Davis

A wise person has great power, and a person of knowledge increases strength.
Proverbs 24:5, The Bible

up control. The transformational para-dox is that by giving up control he/she gains much more control over the quantity and quality of the organiza-tions output than he/she ever could imagine. How? Remember the Sur-vival exercise?

Leaders/managers must delegate the responsibility for change to teams whose members are collectively quali-fied to make effective decisions. In this manner, the process of transformation will move persistently ahead while managers keep their eyes on the short-term successes needed to finance the change.

If this sounds like an extended pro-cess – well, it usually is. Depending on the complexity of the organization, it can take from three to five years to establish new behaviors and generate high-impact results. Beyond this pe-riod, it may take an additional three to five years until the new policies are entrenched in the organization and be-come not the "new" way but "our" way.

When the entrenchment finally oc-curs, the first phase of the transforma-tion process has achieved completion: It has permeated and altered the corpo-rate soul, influencing behaviors, poli-cies and values to such a degree that they are adapted and followed uncon-sciously in a manner – and with a range of benefits – that often surpasses the original intent of the program.

QUESTIONS AND CONSIDERATIONS

1. Have you experienced the traditional approach to change described earlier? How did that process affect you?

_____

_____

_____

_____

_____

_____

_____

2. Have you become familiar with the Catch-22 of corporate change described earlier? What has been your response? What have you done to avoid it?

_____

_____

_____

_____

_____

_____

_____

_____

_____

3. Are you prepared to take the Leap of Faith described earlier? If <u>yes</u> . . . Why? If <u>no</u> . . . what conditions would need to be met before you would take the leap?

_____

_____

_____

_____

_____

_____

_____

_____

_____

_____

CHAPTER 16

Big Ideas

Big Idea #1: The Parable of the Hundredth Monkey and how it applies to organizational change.

Big Idea #2: Form follows function in building a Transformation Steering Team.

Big Idea #3: The Four Key Responsibilities of the Steering Team.
I)Communication.
II)Providing Answers.
III)Action.
IV)Initiating.

CHAPTER 16

Streetcars and Monkeys: A Parable of Transformation.

Throughout the mid- to late-1980s, I designed and facilitated a series of Leadership Development Programs for middle and senior managers of the Toronto Transportation Commission, better known as the TTC. Wherever municipal transportation companies are talked about, the TTC is highly regarded as a well-managed operation (arguably one of the best in the world), and they were determined to maintain their enviable status.

Core Values at the T.T.C.:
Safety
Courtesy
Service

We began each workshop by discussing the direction of the desired transformation and the need for a new leadership paradigm. These sessions became very popular and continued for several years as the program developed and implementation was launched.

During these discussions, I often employed the Fable of the Hundredth Monkey to demonstrate how transformation tended to occur among organizations and sub-cultures. It went like this:

Progress begins a step at a time. There is no sudden leap to greatness.

Scattered across a corner of the South Pacific is a chain of islands inhabited only by a rare species of monkeys. The monkeys survived exclusively on a diet of bananas, which grew in profusion on the islands.

All was well until a time when a typhoon struck the islands, virtually wiping out the banana crop. The vicious winds yanked ripe fruit from the trees and buried it beneath sand and debris. Environmentalists descended on the island to help the monkeys survive. Changing their diet was out of the question. Besides, there was no real shortage of food; most of the bananas were hidden in the sand. But for centuries, the monkeys had lived among and depended upon the banana trees for their food. They were unequipped mentally to change their habits and begin digging in the sand for their meals.

The environmentalists began teaching the monkeys one by one how to locate the bananas, foraging for their food in an entirely new way. It was slow work. If there is such a thing as skepticism among monkeys, it was rampant on these islands. But eventually one or two, and then a handful and eventually a larger group began understanding the lesson and practicing the new skill. Others watched and gradually began mimicking the same techniques.

On each island, the environmentalists noticed a phenomenon. Whenever about a hundred monkeys began locating bananas beneath the sand, the rest followed in a tidal wave of acceptance. The changeover was sudden and dramatic. It often seemed that the hundredth (or so) monkey to adapt the new skill opened the floodgates of change. The Hundredth Monkey – the actual figure is not important here – represented a critical mass that moved the program swiftly to completion.

As a trainer and consultant, I have seen a similar response among employees of corporations dedicated to the

The most successful in the end are those whose success is the result of steady accretion . . . It is the one who carefully advances step by step, with his mind becoming wider and wider – and progressively better able to grasp any theme or situation – persevering in what he knows to be practical, and concentrating his thought upon it, who is bound to succeed in the greatest degree.

Alexander Graham Bell

Success is the sum of small efforts, repeated day in and day out.

Robert Collier

transformation process. This has led to the realization that *you don't have to train or indoctrinate everyone in the organization.* It is only necessary to identify a core group and provide them with the new skills, tools, techniques and attitudes. Once this core group achieves some transformational successes, its behaviors will be copied and by osmosis it will grow into a critical mass; full compliance is virtually assured.

The first teams empowered to deal with the transformation process represent the "seeds" of this core group – adding another reason to base the process on a team structure. It is therefore critical that we create and empower teams, especially the first ones, wisely.

The Steering Team: Form and Function

The transformation process consists of two distinct functions: Steering and Design. Each function can be broken into five individual steps.

For the Steering Function, these steps are:

1. Formation and empowerment of the Steering Team.

2. Establishment and implementation of a system of project nomination.

3. Selection by the Steering Team of the highest priority project from those nominated.

4. Creation of a Mission Statement for each project.

5. Formation of a Design team for each project.

In its early stage it may be desirable for membership on the Steering Team to be drawn from the ranks of senior managers. The positive aspect of this approach is that it sends a powerful message to the organization about the importance of the program. The negative sides are: a) It now becomes a part of the hierarchy and b) It will be caught in the Catch 22 outlined earlier. For these reasons, it is vital that as quickly as possible membership be extended to include representatives from all levels and functions within the organization.

Larger companies will benefit from the establishment of linked Steering Teams at both the corporate and division levels. An effective method of linking the levels is to construct the corporate-level team from chairpersons of the division-level groups.

The quality of your communication determines the quality of your life.

Responsibilities of the Steering Team: #1 Communicate, Communicate, Communicate.

Of all the responsibilities of the Steering Team, communication is foremost. Remember that the very nature of its function – to oversee and manage the first stages of change and transformation – will be disturbing. All change, even that which is needed and welcomed, generates its own tension and stress; neutralizing these side effects demands effective and continuous communication to all and at all levels.

This is an age of organized effort. On every hand we see evidence that organization is the basis of all success, and while other factors enter into the attainment of success, this factor is still one of major importance.

Napoleon Hill

Specific tasks of the Steering Team include, in chronological order:

1. Defining and publishing its Mission Statement.
2. Publishing a membership list.
3. Assigning responsibilities to each member. In this category, sample responsibilities may include:

- Creating effective and appropriate communication vehicles: what, when, where, to whom.
- Formulating the change policy (more about this later).
- Establishing the project selection process.
- Establishing the team selection process.
- Providing resources: training, time spent working on projects, diagnostic support, facilitator support.
- Assuring that project solutions are implemented.
- Establishing methods of evaluating success: progress, performance, management achievements, etc.
- Providing reviews of progress and co-ordination.
- Creating a system of recognition for teams and individuals.
- Agreeing on ways to modify the reward system.

#2 Providing the Answers: First, Anticipate the Questions

Proclaiming a program of change will generate a wide litany of questions from every sector. Instead of waiting

Question:
What do you think is the first requisite for success in your field or any other?
Answer by Thomas A. Edison:
"The ability to apply your physical and mental energies to one problem incessantly without growing weary."

for the questions to be asked, the Steering Team should take a proactive approach by anticipating the questions and formulating the answers in advance.

Here are a few of the questions typically asked, whether articulated aloud to management, discussed among staff or percolating silently through the thoughts of individuals:

- What is the Steering Team's purpose?
- Why does the organization need this change?
- What is the priority of this program, relative to other efforts?
- What jobs will be most affected by this new program, and how?
- Will the people whose jobs are most affected have an opportunity to participate in the planning?
- What steps will be taken, and in what sequence?
- How will the results be measured?
- Who will provide answers to our questions and updates on the progress?

These questions must be anticipated, and answers formulated, prior to implementing the program (another reason to emphasize the role of communications). Delays in providing answers can create uncertainty.

When every physical and mental resource is focused, one's power to solve a problem multiplies tremendously.

Norman Vincent Peale

What do I mean by concentration? I mean focusing totally on the business at hand and commanding your body to do exactly what you want it to do.

Arnold Palmer

#3 Initiating Action: A Guide to Restoring the Soul

With the Steering Team in place and the goals clearly defined, a series of steps must be taken to move towards full implementation.

A. Project Nomination – Cast Your Net Wide.

At the root of every continuous improvement philosophy is the belief that opportunities for improvement can be found in almost every activity undertaken by the organization. Acceptance of that fact leads to the realization that *every individual and job function relating to the company's activity represents a source of insight into critical improvement areas.*

As the fletcher whittles and make straight his arrows, so the master directs his straying thoughts.

Buddha

As a result, project nomination sources should not be limited to the Steering Team – or even to employees generally. They should be sought among customers, non-customers, competitors, suppliers and associates.

All your strength is in your union, All your danger is in discord.

Henry Wadsworth Longfellow

Which objectives deserve your firm's attention? The answer lies, I suggest, among the formal data systems already in place in your organization. These include:

1. *Reports on customer satisfaction/dissatisfaction.* Examine warranty charges, claims, correspondence, returns, dealer comments, etc.

2. *Survey non-customers.* If 20% of the market buys from you, find out why the other 80% doesn't. What can be done about that?

3. *Your own evaluations of competitive quality.* How are the other people stacking up to your performance? What will it take to leap-frog past them?

4. *Sales force reports.* What are they saying about the market's acceptance of your product and service?

5. *Service call reports and field failure analyses.* What problems are being encountered in the field?

6. *Accounting data.* How much does it cost you to have demotivated, non-participative employees?

All of these techniques are used so that they can inform us in answering the transformational question . . . What kind of individuals and teams must we become to: i) satisfy our customers? ii) leap-frog past our competitors? iii) exceed customer expectations in the marketplace? These outcomes now can inform organizational goal setting . . . What must we change within ourselves and our organizations to become this type of person / organization?

Our nominations must always reflect the values of the corporate soul, as represented by individuals who are closely associated with the target area or procedure. It is possible – and dangerous – to nominate revisions in corporate policies or operations which are in direct conflict with these shared values – leading, not surprisingly, to frustration and eventually total failure.

As every divided kingdom falls, so every mind divided between many studies confounds and saps itself.

Leonardo Da Vinci

Reflecting this, Steering Teams should seek nominations from three key sources:

1. An organization wide "Call for Nominations."
2. "Making the Rounds."
3. Steering Team Members themselves.

In a Call for Nominations, the Team invites all personnel to suggest topics, either through the existing management structure or to a designated Steering Team Member.

"Making the Rounds" involves assigning specific departments or procedures to various Team members who talk with key individuals and secure their views and nominations.

Since Team Members are themselves the focal point of data analysis and proposals, they represent an important source of nominations. But they must not be the exclusive well-spring of ideas; it is vital to "cast your nets wide" and see all stakeholders as potential sources of valuable contributions and insights.

Soliciting nominations from the work force carries its own risks, of course. The most dangerous is the expectation by some members of the organization that acceptance of their suggestions will represent a commitment to act upon them. When this is not the case, the response may lead to resentment and cynicism.

Defend against this possibility by stressing the key responsibility of the

Concentrate . . . for the greatest achievements are reserved for the person of single aim, in whom no rival powers divide the empire of the soul.
O. S. Marden

Steering Team for focusing the expenditure of all limited resources by prioritizing all suggestions. While every nomination is to receive serious consideration, only those meeting the top levels of criteria in terms of practicality ("Is it do-able?") and reasonable reward ("What's the bang for our buck?") will be addressed at the outset. Others will be re-evaluated at a future date, preferably once or twice per year.

It would be helpful for the Steering Team to publish its priority-setting criteria along with all the ideas nominated so that contributors can better understand the decision process and allow it to inform their future suggestions.

B. Project Selection – Criteria for Now and Thereafter.

A critical early step is for the Steering Team to screen all nominations and choose carefully those projects to be tackled.

But first, a Major Commandment must be respected:

Decisions regarding the selection of the first projects will set the tone for the entire process . . . therefore . . . choose wisely.

Knowledge comes but wisdom lingers.
Alfred Lord Tennyson

Wisdom is knowledge which has become a part of one's being.
O. S. Marden

First impressions are as critical in achieving success in a change management program as they are in relationships. Anything less than near-total success in the first project or two will kindle the fires of cynicism and discomfort in various groups and individuals – even in those who fully subscribe to the shared corporate spirit.

Success is . . . the progressive realization of a worthy goal.

It may be wiser to succeed at a small chunk of a significant problem than to completely eliminate an unimportant one.

The experience gathered from books, though often valuable, is but the nature of learning: whereas the experience gained is of the nature of wisdom . . .
Samuel Smiles

Does this mean the first few projects to be tackled should be "no-brainers"? Absolutely not! – Solving a problem whose remedy has been evident for years will impress no one. Instead, gauge the project against these four qualifications:

1. *It should represent a chronic problem*. Tackling a long-standing challenge will impress everyone that you're serious about change and not merely yearning for it.

2. *Its solution should be feasible*. Choose a project with practical possibilities for achieving success <u>within a few months</u>.

3. *It should represent a significant advance*. Reducing the firm's consumption of paper clips may be feasible and beneficial, but it impresses few. Make sure the project generates <u>a major impact</u> on everyone.

4. *Results must be measurable*, ideally in financial as well as in technological, quality and social dimensions.

The goal is to achieve at least reasonable success on a project whose importance is widely recognized . . . and whose benefits are obvious to every employee.

With the first success or two on the score sheet, the criteria for future projects will shift to other qualities.

After the impact of the first few projects has been felt, the selection process encompasses other measures. Now the

Steering Team begins to search for projects which:

1. <u>Generate substantial returns on investment</u>. All things being equal, this becomes the most decisive factor. In some cases, such as corporate image management and new employee induction and training, it may be difficult to precisely measure incremental improvements, and the Steering Team may need to co-opt specific managers or the entire Management Team to assist in the priority setting process. Projects should include two broad types: i) ways to increase quality, ii) ways to decrease cost.

2. <u>Achieve the largest total impact</u>. Given time and facilities, a choice may have to be made between either one major project or several smaller ones critical to the improvement process. A rational formula for assessing the total impact should be developed and applied.

3. <u>Represent a need for urgent solution</u>. Some projects may be fast-tracked to the front of the line in response to other factors. Product and employee safety, staff morale and customer service – are a few examples.

4. <u>May be tackled with existing technology and facilities</u>. Projects whose solution can be found amid existing technology or facilities may take precedence over those requiring extensive research or in-

vestment in new equipment, systems or personnel.

5. <u>Respond to developing or steady growth in the product cycle</u>. Most organizations deal with products at various stages in their life cycle. It's obvious that projects dealing with products whose greatest growth period is yet to be achieved should take precedence over mature or declining products.

6. <u>Will encounter low resistance to change</u>. Projects that can be expected to receive a favorable reception should take precedence over those which may encounter resistance from labor unions, intransigent managers and other potential barriers.

Keep Your Eyes on the Prize

In the midst of the above, it is so easy to lose sight of our purpose: To build an organization (body) around a compelling set of values (soul).

This purpose/mission must be considered constantly because each project you select must serve this purpose and embody these values:

1. Does this project strengthen us as an organization?
2. Does this project help us to better live out our values?

C. Project Mission Statements: Keep It Simple Soldier.

They've been around for years and may have generated their own degree

A Mission is a description of a desired state of affairs that fuels motivation, clarifies direction and triggers action.

A goal is a general statement of intent or direction. e.g., My goal is to be an effective communicator.

An Objective is a specific statement of <u>what</u> results will be achieved <u>when</u>.

Objectives should be written in the future-perfect tense. I.e., As if it's already done.

Objectives tell <u>what</u> not <u>how</u>.

of skepticism. But the value of cogent, effective Mission Statements in determining the appropriateness of actions and maintaining a clear focus on objectives cannot be over-estimated.

First rule: Keep the original draft simple. Here are a few samples of effective Project Mission Statements:

- Reduce the number of incorrect invoices sent to clients.
- Reduce the time needed for client service.
- Reduce the volume of conveyor spillage.

As the Team gains confidence and experience, Mission Statements can be expanded to encompass a wider range of activities or more precisely identify goals and activities.

Second rule: Accompany each Mission Statement with SMART objectives, as in:

Specific

Measurable

Agreed-on

Realistic

Timely

As an example of a SMART objective:

By September 15th, we will have reduced incorrect client invoices by 15%.

Once the Mission Statement and SMART objectives are established, they must be officially published and distributed to all stakeholders, conveying both legitimacy and commitment; in effect, these missions, goals and objectives become part of the corporate business plan and another element in the shared corporate spirit.

QUESTIONS AND CONSIDERATIONS:

1. What is the meaning and application of the Parable of the Hundredth Monkey?

1. ....

2. ....

3. ....

2. What are the major responsibilities of the Steering Team?

1. ....

2. ....

3. ....

3. Why is it critical to choose the first projects wisely?

....

....

....

....

....

....

....

....

4. What are the four most important criteria of the first projects?

1. _____

2. _____

3. _____

4. _____

CHAPTER 17

Big Ideas

In this chapter you will find many practical tips and guidelines for ensuring the success of your Project Design Teams.

Big Idea #1: The key function of a Design Team.

Big Idea #2: Definitions and examples of key planning terms such as:
Missions.
Goals.
Objectives.

Big Idea #3: Who should sit on a particular Design Team?

Big Idea #4: The role of a team charter.

Big Idea #5: The role of Team Facilitators and Sponsors.

CHAPTER 17

Empowered Design Teams: The Body and Soul of the Transformation Process.

The purpose of the Steering Team is to steer, to look ahead, identify the long term results or end points and then to ensure that all resources are focused on getting us there.

Our Goal is the total participation of all stakeholders in the continuous improvement of all aspects of the business.

The Objective – by the end of year 1 to have had the active participation of every stakeholder in the Steering Team or in a Design Team.

There is no known upper limit to the quality and productivity gains possible when a highly motivated and focused team tackles a project.

Each project to be tackled deserves its own Project Design team. Membership in individual Project Design teams may – and almost certainly will – overlap.

Delegate responsibility for successful completion of a project to synergistic problem solving teams of five to seven persons. Their function is to *design solutions and carry out actions to ensure that desired improvements are implemented.*

Project Design teams embody both the spirit and action of corporate change, and their duties can be categorized as parts of the overall corporate body, carrying out actions on behalf of the corporate soul.

They are the heart of the activity. All actions center around their decisions and energy; when Project Design teams function poorly or not at all, the process of change withers and dies.

They are the brains of the function. By applying wisdom, intelligence, deductive reasoning, observation and perception, Project Design teams guide the transformation process through all the inevitable twists and challenges toward successful completion.

They are the hands and feet of the process. Successful Project Design teams do not restrict themselves to meeting

What do we live for, if it is not to make life less difficult for each other?

George Eliot

We cannot live only for ourselves. A thousand fibers connect us with our fellow-men.

Herman Melville

Coming together is a beginning; keeping together progress; working together is success.

Henry Ford

Experience proves that the most effective organization mechanisms for dealing with interdepartmental problems are inter-departmental teams.

rooms and memos. They reach out to all locations within the organization, taking a "hands-on" approach. In the parlance of training and management, they literally "walk the talk."

Design Team Membership: Drafting a Championship Contender

Earlier, I demonstrated the strength of teams versus the activities of individuals. Once the transformation process is launched, the value of teams grows even more pronounced. Why? *Because the major transformation problems faced by all organizations are interdepartmental in nature.*

Even when the symptoms of a problem may be evident exclusively in one department, the effects are inevitably transmitted throughout several levels of the organization. Treating any problem in isolation – whether it's medical, mechanical or organizational – restricts the degree of total success achieved. Problems in the shipping department, for example, will be felt throughout the rest of the company as well – and that makes the problem an interdepartmental one.

More important, solutions often are found elsewhere in the organization even when the problem is confined to an (apparently) isolated area. Small procedural changes in production, scheduling, sales, accounting and elsewhere can be made to positively affect activities in shipping without disrupting any other aspect of the organization.

Apart from this need for interdepartmental representation, what other criteria are necessary for team membership? The answer lies in a number of questions to be addressed:

- Which departments are to be represented on the team (see above)?
- From what levels of the hierarchy should members be drawn?
- Which individuals are available to be recruited onto the team?

To determine team representation by departments, begin by identifying four groups and include at least one member from each. The groups are:

The broader the vision, the more accurate the definition, the more satisfying the result.

1. The subject department – the one which will be the focus of the transformation activity.
2. The contributing departments – areas where at least part of the cause may originate.
3. The remedial departments – areas in the organization where potential solutions may be found. (Note: Stress the potential aspects; an effective transformation team will almost certainly uncover surprising, unexpected sources of causes and remedies).
4. The diagnostic departments – groups who, when needed, can assemble and analyze data to measure success.

Team Rights and Responsibilities

Change generates discomfort and concern, no matter how well-intentioned and well-managed the process may be.

With that in mind, it's important that team membership and goals be identified, published and circulated among all members of the organization. In addition to reducing discomfort levels to some degree, generating wide awareness of the program assigns group responsibility and establishes legitimacy for the team, its members and its actions.

Publication also bestows specific rights on the team, including:

- The right to hold meetings, publish minutes and reports and take specific actions within their areas of responsibility.

- The right to request contributions from individuals and departments outside the team itself.

- The right to request information and data related to the project.

Much of the above will be defined by the Project Mission Statement, prepared by the Transformation Steering Team and finalized/adopted by each Project Design Team.

But more than a Mission Statement is needed to lend true legitimacy to team activities.

We have forty million rea-sons for failure, but not a single excuse.
Rudyard Kipling

No alibi will save you from accepting the responsi-bility . . .
Napoleon Hill

The grand aim of all sci-ence is to cover the greatest number of em-pirical facts by logical de-duction from the smallest number of hypotheses or axioms.
Albert Einstein

Team Charters: Impersonal Supervision for Team Activities

The most effective teams frequently have no personal "boss." A Chairper-son may be chosen to both share the responsibilities of all members as well as conduct specific functions such as meeting scheduling, etc., and appoint a secretary to record minutes and re-ports. But the Chairperson's role is not one of supervision.

Teams are supervised by the con-tents of the Mission Statement and Team Charter. The latter defines activ-ities of the Team and may include (but not be restricted to) such activities as:

- Analyzing symptoms of the prob-lem.
- Theorizing the causes.
- Testing the theories.
- Establishing causes.
- Proposing remedies.
- Testing remedies under operating conditions.
- Evaluating the tests.
- Establishing controls to maintain the gains.

Facilitators: Team Process Specialists

Early in the transformation process, Steering Teams will benefit from the assistance of Facilitators – specialists who have undergone training and who accept this role as a part-time assignment in addition to their normal responsibilities.

Among the functions of Team Facilitators are:

1. Communications Channel: the Facilitator functions as a communications link between teams, management staff and others who may not be represented on the team. Facilitators may serve several teams and can act as a conduit for successful – and less than successful – experiences and techniques. The achievements of other teams will serve to inspire members engaged in the overall transformation process; the miscues and small failures of other teams will console these same members when they encounter similar barriers that appear to defy solution.

2. Team Builder: The Facilitator's training focuses on skills and techniques to guide members towards effective teamwork practices (outlined earlier). The facilitator in a sense "owns the process" while the team members "own the content." It is his/her job to ensure that the team uses the most efficient and effective problem solving, decision making, brainstorming tools and techniques at the appropriate times.

3. Focusing and Directing: At one time or another virtually all teams become "bogged down" without realizing it, or without knowing how to break the impasse. An effec-

The criterion of simplicity requires that the minimum number of assumptions be postulated.
Albert Low

Less is more.
Robert Browning

Part of my job is to train people to break down an involved question into a series of simple matters. Then we can all act intelligently.
Richard Deupree

tive Facilitator can take a detached view and clearly recognize the true location of the problem – such as a Project Mission statement which is too broad or vaguely defined, or a department or function whose participation is critical to the team's success but who is not represented on the team.

5. <u>Assist the Chair:</u> While the Facilitator is not a formal team member (and, as a result, should avoid becoming involved in substantive decisions or activities), he or she can aid the chairperson in two ways:

- Stimulating Attendance – Most non-attendance is due to conflicts on members' time; the solution may lie with a discussion between the Facilitator and the member's supervisor.

- Conflict Resolution between team members – Conflict may exist or arise between team members, or between the team and its Chairperson. A skilled Facilitator will recognize these conflicts and find ways to redirect the energy into constructive channels. (This is usually achieved outside of the team meeting atmosphere.)

6. <u>Measuring and Reporting Progress:</u> At the outset, teams often have difficulty generating useful reports and various measurements. Facilitators can be helpful in drafting these reports into cogent, meaningful documents. Remember that the Facilitator's roles are most critical during the start-up period. As Proj-

We have met the enemy . . . and they is us.
Pogo
Walt Kelly

Genius is the ability to reduce the complicated to the simple.
C. W. Ceram

First say to yourself what you would be; and then do what you have to do.
Epictetus

ect teams and their members grow more secure in their duties, the Facilitator should gradually withdraw his or her services, acting only when requested.

A Word from our "Sponsor"

Since Project Design Teams are unattached to the organization's traditional chain of command, this can create a handicap in the event of an unexpected impasse. To counter this, consider assigning team members or senior managers to be sponsors (or "champions") for specific projects, with direct access to top management levels in the hierarchy.

Surrounding these mechanical activities is the presence of that elusive corporate soul which – much like the earth's atmosphere; though transparent, tasteless, colorless and odorless, makes possible life as we know it.

This spirit, in a positive sense, enables each step of this Design process and links it in a seemless circle with all that we've discussed so far and will attempt to summarize in our final chapter.

QUESTIONS AND CONTEMPLATIONS

1. What is the role of the Steering Team compared to that of the Design Team?

2. Why is it important for every team to have a Mission Statement as well as a set of written Goals and Objectives?

3. What are the three most important criteria for choosing who should sit on a Design Team?

CHAPTER 18

Big Ideas

Big Idea #1: Summarize the Ten Step Transformation Process.

Big Idea #2: Re-Emphasize the critical need for teamwork.

Big Idea #3: Point out the "continuous growth" aspect of strongly "soulful" organizations.

Big Idea #4: Provide two final illustrations which, I hope, make a strong case for concentrating on building an organization with a soul as well as a body.

CHAPTER 18

Ten Steps to Transforming the Body and Soul of Your Organization

Whatever we plant in our subconscious mind and nourish with emotion will one day become a reality.

Earl Nightingale

The idea is to make decisions and act on them – to decide what is important to accomplish, to decide how something can best be accomplished, to find time to work at it and to get it done.

Karen Kakascik

Just to review:

- Effective change cannot be achieved without the participation of teams representing a wide range of departments and functions within the organization.

- Two types of teams are necessary to complete the transformation process: Steering Teams and Design Teams.

- Team functions must be defined, communicated and ultimately legitimized through the use of Mission Statements and Team Charters.

- Teams elect a Chairperson to carry out administrative duties, but they operate most effectively without a supervisor.

- At the outset, teams rely on a trained Facilitator whose role is to advise in terms of internal operation without playing an active role in carrying out team duties. As the team gains experience and confidence, the Facilitator gradually withdraws.

- The stronger the shared corporate spirit, the more effective the teams and the more successful the transformation process.

Each team group takes a five-step approach to the transformation process, as described earlier. To summarize:

Five Steps to Transformation by the Steering Team

STEP 1: The steering team is formed and empowered by senior management.

STEP 2: A system of project nomination is established and implemented.

STEP 3: The Steering Team selects the highest priority projects from among those nominated.

STEP 4: The Steering Team creates a Mission Statement for each project.

STEP 5: A Design Team is created for each selected project.

Five Steps to Transformation by the Design Team

STEP 1: The Design Team meets to review, revise and adopt the Mission Statement.

STEP 2: The Design Team brainstorms as many ideas as possible to achieve its mission.

STEP 3: The team selects three to five key action steps and assigns team members and sub-teams to carry out the actions.

STEP 4: Team members take action according to their assignments.

STEP 5: Actions are evaluated, modified and reapplied if necessary; if successful, another level of transformation is identified, and steps 2 and 5 are repeated.

All effective management begins with planning.

In all planning you make a list and you set priorities.

To review priorities ask the question: What's the best use of our time right now?
Alan Lakein

Is what we're doing or about to do getting us closer to our objective?

You can't dig a hole in a new place by digging the same hole deeper.
Edward de Bono

He who every morning plans the transactions of the day and follows out that plan, carries a thread that will be a guide through the labyrinth of the most busy life.

Victor Hugo

The deepest principle in human nature is the craving to be appreciated.

William James

Good, the more communicated, more abundant grows.

John Milton

At first glance, the rather mechanical "Ten Steps" approach may appear to have little to do with the existence and nurturing of a corporate soul. In fact, the more powerful the presence of an over-riding spirit reflecting a shared sense of values, the more smoothly these step-by-step functions will occur and the more effective the teamwork required to complete the process.

It's easy to comprehend, it seems to me, how a strong, vibrant corporate soul will enable the team-based transformation process to succeed. In a corporation lacking soul, team membership will be viewed as onerous, something to do to keep "the people upstairs" happy. In an organization with a strong spirit of shared goals and achievement, team membership will be recognized for what it is: empowerment and recognition, an opportunity to shape one's future job satisfaction.

Moreover, strongly "soulful" organizations actively search for an opportunity to renew their sense of spirit while retaining the traditions which represent the foundation of their success. These organizations, both within and beyond the corporate world, recognize the need to periodically renew themselves within the framework of society *because no organization can resist for long the continuing reassessment and realignment of the society which they serve.* To resist change completely is like aquatic life that is unable to cope with rising or falling water temperatures – without adaptation, it will become ex-

The greatest mistake is to resist change.

Every dogma has its day.
Abraham Rotstein

tinct. The balancing act, of course, is to adapt to changing conditions while retaining the qualities which led to your success in the first place. But isn't that the basis of successful business management in the first place? Tropical fish whose water gradually drops a few degrees in temperature evolve into fish who can survive in cooler water; they do not change into seals and walruses. Similarly, corporations who succeed in one product category first attempt to modify their product category to meet changing tastes, building on established strength. Except when no other recourse is possible, food companies do not become airlines and computer firms do not switch to automotive parts manufacturing.

And the stronger the corporate soul, the more easily adjustments are made when working within established and widely-cherished values.

Think of your own experiences with organizations whose existence is based on a shared spiritual context.

Over the past few decades, organized religion has begun reaching out to groups and sub-cultures whose existence was once either ignored, denied or even attacked. Gays, people of color and faiths based upon differing beliefs were all, within the memory of most adults today, rejected by some religious groups. Attitudes have changed, but only over an extended period of time and in the face of conflicts or challenges which threatened to wound or weaken the organization in question.

In religious groups, this change can take place over an extended period of time, gradually reflecting the slowly adjusted perceptions of its members and leaders. In the business world, which is much less forgiving and much faster paced, the organization would have withered and died, or succumbed to mergers and takeovers, much earlier.

Stepping onto some admittedly thin ice, I'm prepared to go further and address groups in this category which have resisted change – at a price.

The Islamic religion provides its members with great spiritual strength. Although I am not a religious scholar, I recognize that the teachings of Mohammed reflect many of the values of Christ. Indeed, Muslims, Christians and Jews alike are referred to by Islamic followers as "People of the Book" – a recognition that members of all three groups accept belief in one deity.

At the end of this current millennium, the Islamic religion in several countries is being torn in several directions. In countries such as Iran and Afghanistan, actions are taken which, in the opinion of scholars far more conversant with Islamic beliefs than I am, are in conflict with the basic tenets of their beliefs.

No one knows where this will lead, but it's clear to me, as I'm sure it is to you, that much of the tension and resulting violence arises not from the values and goals of the religion itself but of *its inability to deal with change that occurs around it.*

Societies change. Values are adjusted. People perceive their place and role in life differently as time passes. This is neither A Good Thing nor A Bad Thing. Good or bad, society reinvents itself generation by generation, and the process must be dealt with.

Not all change in organized religion has produced positive aspects; I can listen to arguments on both sides of the question regarding the place of Latin in Roman Catholic liturgy, for example, and appreciate the value of each.

But I believe one thing is clear, whatever the context:

Any change that strengthens the spirit strengthens the organization, and the stronger this spirit, the more easily the organization adapts to change.

The hard knocks of the 1990s have seen corporations abandon many of the pillars supporting a sense of corporate soul. Who needs a soul when "Chainsaw" Albert J. Dunlap can earn $116 000 a day (based on his 18-month tenure at Scott Paper) for reducing the staff of a 117-year-old company by 35% before selling the firm to its rival for $9.4 billion?* In his self-serving biography, Dunlap fails to recognize the following key points:

A day spent without beauty, without the contemplation of mystery, or without the search for truth or perfection is a poverty-stricken day, and a succession of such days is fatal to human life.

Lewis Mumford

Mean Business: How I Save Bad Companies and Make Good Companies Great (Time Books)

- The company he "saved" was the second-largest in its market and the world leader in its product category.
- Many initiatives which "saved" the company were underway when Dunlap arrived.
- Dunlap cut R & D costs – the basis of much of Scott's past success – in half and dismissed 60% of its R & D staff. As a result, Scott is currently losing market share in all three of its product categories.
- He claims he "saved" Scott Paper by causing almost 12 000 employees to lose their jobs before selling the firm to its key competitor. Is that salvation, savagery or is it surrender?
- Dunlap states that a CEO's only responsibility is to the company's shareholders. In the case of Scott Paper at least, he is partially correct; as one of the firms' major shareholders he profited to the tune of almost $100 million in his sale of the firm to its competitor. And don't employees, who usually depend on the firm for 100% of their income, have as great a stake in its success as shareholders, whose dependence on the firm is almost always a small portion of their total net worth?

To add even greater gall, Dunlap has proclaimed: *"I'm a superstar in my field, much like Michael Jordan in basketball and Bruce Springsteen in rock and roll."*

Mr. Dunlap is entitled to his high opinion of himself.

What is hateful to you, do not do to your neighbor. That is the whole Torah. The rest is commentary. Go and study.
Babylonian Talmud

A few years ago, Lily Tomlin made a wry comment on aspects of cut-throat business. "The trouble with being in a rat-race," she said, "is that, even if you win it, you're still a rat."

No one said it would be easy.

Managing a successful company is rarely easy, because the solutions to challenges and problems are rarely simple.

But it can be fun, and it can be rewarding in ways that are far beyond the measure of a favorable stock option or a luxury corner office.

The secret lies in seeking, finding, touching and enriching the corporate BODY AND SOUL of your organization.

Enjoy the journey!

One final question. One last consideration.

What are you going to do about it?

My best wishes to you.

May your journey make you strong.